Rethinking Biblical Divorce

Let Scripture Be Your Guide

James Sander

Linda Sander

Elena Hensley

Cover design by Caleb Hensley

Contents

Introduction

Why would anyone write another book about divorce? And why would anyone read another book about divorce?

A day came when the question of divorce became more than a hypothetical discussion for us, and we realized we needed to make a careful study to see what Scripture actually teaches about the topic. Our book is the result of several years of diligent Bible study about divorce. What we found is not what we expected, and we want to share what we have learned.

That leads to the question why would anyone *read* another book about divorce? Certainly, another book about divorce would need to offer new insights that would benefit the reader. This book does offer new insights, ones that will free readers from the guilt, confusion, and frustration that are prevalent in the church today. We develop these insights by using two simple tools.

The first tool is **context**. We may think that what we learned about divorce in the past was based on considering "the divorce verses" in their context, but as this book examines verses about divorce, we will see that very often this has not been the case. Keeping the divorce verses in context will lengthen our discussion, but it is fundamental and indispensable for developing an accurate understanding of what Scripture does and does not teach about divorce. This book considers these verses in their context.

The second tool is an **understanding of a few key Greek words**, which are invaluable for gaining a correct understanding of these verses. There is no need to be apprehensive about these words as they are straightforward and simple to apply. They are also indispensable to grasp what Scripture teaches about divorce.

In each New Testament passage about divorce, both tools–context and a Greek word or two–will be the greatest help to discover new insights into Scriptural teaching about divorce and will make reading this book worthwhile.

Our book begins with Matthew 5:31-32 as these are the most familiar verses in the Bible about divorce; most theories and discussions about divorce start here. We find that context requires a deeper look, and we learn one Greek word that will be invaluable in understanding Jesus' point.

Part II examines the two other times Jesus mentions divorce. Three Greek words are put to use, and we explain how the context of the Pharisees' confrontation with Jesus and his later explanation to his disciples determines the meaning.

Part III discusses abuse in marriage and we find that two Greek words dramatically affect our understanding of Scripture's teaching about this subject. We find that the Bible specifically and clearly addresses abuse, and we discover how the church is commanded to deal with abusers.

Part IV considers 1 Corinthians 7. We keep Paul's words about divorce in context and put to use two Greek words that help make sense of his words.

In Part V, we quickly look at Malachi 2:16 and the familiar phrase, "I hate divorce."

Part VI concludes the book with a discussion of some practical ideas to strengthen our marriages and to help our marriages last. Appendices add informative background and insights.

Some may suppose there is no need to read another book about divorce. If you have already settled on a position, you will find fresh insights in this book that are biblically based, and we encourage you to consider what we have to say. Prepare to let Scripture be your guide as we go on this journey.

PART I

One of the Most Misunderstood Passages in Scripture

1 | The Exception Clause and Two Context Mistakes

The first passage we will consider in our discussion about divorce is Matthew 5:31-32, which is part of Matthew's account of Jesus' Sermon on the Mount. This passage has been the cornerstone of the church's stand on divorce for many centuries; however, as we take time to examine whether we have interpreted these verses correctly, we will see that Jesus' purpose is not to give us rules for divorce. Rather, as we work through Part I, we will see Jesus' purpose is to show our need to have him satisfy God's perfect righteousness for us.

The verses say,

It was also said, 'Whoever divorces his wife, let him give her a certificate of divorce." But I say to you that everyone who divorces his wife, except for the ground of sexual immorality, makes her commit adultery, and whoever marries a divorced woman commits adultery. (Matthew 5:31-32)[1]

The Exception Clause

These two verses seem straightforward and are enough to convince many in the church that there is only one allowable reason to divorce and/or remarry—sexual immorality. This thought is derived from the phrase "except for the ground of sexual immorality," a three-word phrase in the Greek, *"parektos logou porneias."*

The phrase "except for the ground of sexual immorality" has taken on its own importance, even having a label or designation assigned to it—it is sometimes called the *Exception Clause*. The idea behind the Exception Clause is that a person cannot divorce

---

[1] Unless otherwise noted, Scripture verses are from the English Standard Version (ESV).

and/or remarry *except* if he or she meets the condition stated. Many sermons and books are devoted to these two verses and to the Exception Clause.

The church has various interpretations of this phrase. While we will provide our interpretation later, at this point we simply list common opinions about the meaning of the phrase (some differences may be subtle):[2]

- Jesus meant, "If my spouse did not commit adultery and I divorce, I commit adultery."

- Jesus meant, "If I committed adultery in my marriage and then I divorce, I cannot remarry."

- Jesus meant, "I can divorce only if my spouse was sexually immoral, but Jesus did not mean it is okay for me to remarry."

- Jesus meant, "I can divorce only if my spouse was immoral, and Jesus also meant that in that situation it is okay for me to remarry."

- Jesus meant, "One reason I can divorce is if my spouse was immoral, but I can remarry only if the reason for the divorce was due to immorality on the part of my spouse."

- Jesus' focus was not on divorce but on remarriage and simply meant, "I can remarry only if the divorce was due to immorality on the part of my spouse."

These common interpretations of Matthew 5:31-32 all have profound implications for our lives. Not every church holds to one of these interpretations, but many do. How do we decide what Jesus meant? As we continue our study in Part I, we will see that two tools, context and one Greek word, will guide us and will reveal Jesus' meaning and purpose for this phrase.

---

[2] We are not concerned at this point about making a distinction between the words adultery and sexual immorality.

Two Context Mistakes
That Send Us Down the Wrong Path

Most of us care deeply about adhering to the context of every Scripture passage we study. This is why we participate in Bible studies, and it is why our pastors and teachers spend so much time preparing sermons and lessons. It is very important to us. If this describes you, this book will likely be refreshing in its handling of context. Although we assume most studies about divorce have adhered to the context, many well-known teachings on Matthew 5:31-32 contain two context mistakes.

The First Context Mistake

Verses 31-32 of Matthew 5 were not given in isolation. They are part of the larger discourse of Matthew 5:17-48, which itself is part of the Sermon on the Mount.

To properly grasp Matthew 5:31-32, we need to understand how these verses fit within their larger discourse, which means reviewing the other illustrations that lead up to and follow after these familiar verses about divorce. If we wonder what these other verses have to do with it and why we cannot examine just the two verses that mention divorce, it is because of the great value we all put on understanding Scripture in light of its context, and along with this, we understand error often comes when we make an application from an isolated text. Thus, the entire context will be considered.

Although we might whole-heartedly agree with the principle of keeping verses in their context, we often handle verses 31-32 very differently from the verses preceding and following them. Many of us make an abrupt change in our thinking when we come to verses 31-32, and without realizing it, we remove the verses from the context of Jesus' other examples and apply them differently. Although often unintentional, this treatment of verses 31-32 inevitably leads to an error in understanding and application.

As we follow this thought, we will see that by removing verses 31-32 from their surrounding context, we diminish, and possibly even miss entirely, one of the greatest salvation messages in Scripture.

The Second Context Mistake

Some may think since Jesus also mentioned divorce in other passages in the gospels (Matthew 19:9, Mark 10:11-12, Luke 16:18), they should be included with the discussion of Matthew 5:31-22. This is a good thought because it does seem that way at a cursory glance, and these passages will be addressed in this book. However, they have a different context, and it is of the utmost importance that we keep all Scripture in context.

The second context mistake is inappropriately combining Matthew 5:31-32 with other gospel verses simply because Jesus also mentions divorce in those verses. However, just because two sets of verses use similar wording, it does not necessarily follow they have the same meaning and intent. For example, if someone says, "You should wear black," the meaning of these words will vary greatly depending on the context. The words would be helpful if said to someone going to a funeral or a formal dinner, the words would be sarcastic if said to a malcontent, and the words would be a compliment if they meant the person looks good in black. The same words might be spoken, but the meaning and intent would be quite different depending on the context.

This is the case with these other passages that mention divorce. They are in a completely different context than Matthew 5:31-32. The differences in contexts are easily seen in the following table. (Jesus' mention of divorce in the Luke passage is not included in the following table because the context is not as clearly identifiable in Luke. It is not clear, for example, to whom Jesus made the statements and if there was any reaction.) Scripture passages mentioned in the following chart can be found, with their context, in Appendix F.

Differences in the Contexts of Verses
Where Jesus Mentions Divorce

To the Crowds During the Sermon on the Mount Matthew 5:31-32	To the Pharisees When They Confronted Jesus Matthew 19:3-9/Mark 10:2-9	To The Disciples Later in a House Matthew 19:10-12/Mark 10:10-12
These verses are part of the Sermon on the Mount	These verses are not part of the Sermon on the Mount (nor part of any of Jesus' discourses)	These verses record what Jesus said to the disciples privately after the confrontation with the Pharisees
Jesus initiated the sermon	The Pharisees initiated the confrontation	The disciples asked a question that arose from the confrontation
Jesus sat down to speak and was intentional about a specific message	Jesus was responding to the Pharisees purposeful attempt to trap him	Jesus responded to the disciples' question about application
Jesus' audience was a receptive crowd	Jesus' audience was the antagonistic Pharisees	Jesus' audience was his disciples
The crowd recognized Jesus' authority, and realized it was an authority unlike their other teachers	The Pharisees were trying to undermine Jesus' authority	The disciples recognized Jesus' authority and were ready to learn and apply his teaching

Jesus' confrontation with the Pharisees not only has a completely different context than the Sermon on the Mount, but as we can see from the table, the context is nearly the opposite. Accordingly, we should not use his words to the Pharisees to determine the meaning of Matthew 5:31-32. Similarly, the context of Jesus' comment to the disciples is very different from the other two contexts. Jesus' explanation to his disciples was a response to their question about how to apply the comments he made during the confrontation with the Pharisees.

These other verses are essential to a complete understanding of divorce, so we will look at them on their own in Part II. But at this point, we can see why it is critical we do not muddle the discussion of Matthew 5:31-32 with verses that are significantly different in context. Keeping the verses in context will lead us on the clearest path to understand what the Bible says about divorce.

To summarize, the **first context mistake** occurs when we remove verses 31-32 from the surrounding verses of Matthew 5:17-48 and deal with them differently than the rest of that passage. The **second context mistake** is inappropriately combining Matthew 5:31-32 with other verses in other passages simply because these other verses use similar wording about divorce.

"Of course we shouldn't make these two context mistakes! Who would?"

This question tells us that the discussion about these two context mistakes is more profound than what first appears. The fact is, when it comes to teaching about divorce, very few guard against these two mistakes. Without seeming to be aware of it, it is the norm to hear a teacher jump from one passage to another, combining verses that are in different contexts or omitting the context that the verses are in.

Indeed, these two context mistakes occur so frequently, that it is surprising when they do not occur! As we work our way through the Scriptures that have to do with divorce, take note of the very different contexts in which the verses are found. You will be able to have your guard up for these two context mistakes when you hear teaching about divorce.

Now we are ready to begin considering the passage itself, but first, it will be good to read all of Matthew 5:17-48 (found in Appendix F) before continuing further.

The Structure of Matthew 5:17-48

"Bookend" Verses Indicate One Teaching in One Passage

Matthew 5:17-48 has a noticeable starting point and ending point, which is why it is identified as a distinct passage. We should pay attention to how the passage begins and ends, and that is what we will do first. The beginning verses of this passage, 17-20, and the last verse, verse 48, are the bookends to this passage. They say,

Do not think that I have come to abolish the Law or the Prophets; I have not come to abolish them but to fulfill them. For truly, I say to you, until heaven and earth pass away, not an iota, not a dot, will pass from the Law until all is accomplished. Therefore whoever relaxes one of the least of these commandments and teaches others to do the same will be called least in the kingdom of heaven, but whoever does them and teaches them will be called great in the kingdom of heaven. For I tell you, unless your righteousness exceeds that of the scribes and Pharisees, you will never enter the kingdom of heaven.   (Matthew 5:17-20)

You therefore must be perfect, as your heavenly Father is perfect.   (Matthew 5:48)

These two sets of verses are markers for the beginning and end of the passage showing us that in Matthew 5:17-48 Jesus has a specific message for us to hear—he seems to be saying that not only is a surpassing righteousness required, perfection itself is expected. We will consider the verses again in Chapter 4, but for now it is important to see how they help tie one passage together.

Common Structure of the Verses In Between the Bookends

Verses 21-47 are in between the bookends and they follow a definite structure that we must identify in order to grasp Jesus' point. This passage divides into six parts and each is marked by a traditional command that was well-known to the original audience.[3]

Jesus said, *You have heard that it was said,*

- *Do not murder.* (v. 21)
- *Do not commit adultery.* (v. 27)
- *Whoever divorces his wife must give her a certificate of divorce.* (v. 31)
- *Do not swear falsely.* (v. 33)
- *An eye for an eye and a tooth for a tooth.* (v. 38)
- *Love your neighbor (and hate your enemies).*[4] (v. 43)

From Old Testament times, the Jewish people understood these six "You have heard" statements to be commands of the law.

Jesus then follows each Old Testament command with his own additional comments. It is these additional comments that shed light on Jesus' point in the passage and help us understand the purpose of his teaching, not only in each individual statement, but in the whole passage. In fact, Jesus' words in the "but I say to you" part of his statement *reveal his point*.

We will use the following chart to organize each statement:

---

[3] Exodus 20:13, Exodus 20:14, Exodus 21:24, Deuteronomy 24:1-4, Leviticus 19:18, Number 30:2. It might not seem clear to us when we read Deuteronomy 24:1-4 in our English Bibles that it was a command to give a certificate of divorce, but Jesus makes it clear—the Greek used in Matthew 5:31 for "give" is *dotō*, a command in the Greek.

[4] "Hate your enemies" is not an Old Testament command but was perhaps added from David's words in Psalm 139:21-22, "Do I not hate those who hate you, O LORD? And do I not loathe those who rise up against you? I hate them with complete hatred; I count them my enemies." Although only the first part, "Love your neighbor," is commanded in Scripture, since the people held to the second part, Jesus used it in his teaching.

The Six "You Have Heard" Statements with Jesus' Additional Comments

O. T. Commands	Jesus' Additional Comments
Do not murder. (verse 21)	Whoever is angry with his brother is liable to the judgment, whoever insults his brother will be liable to the council, and whoever says, "you fool!" will be liable to the hell of fire. (verses 22-26)
Do not commit adultery. (verse 27)	When a man looks lustfully at a woman, he commits adultery with her in his heart. If our right eye causes us to sin, we should tear it out, and if our right hand causes us to sin, we should cut it off. (verses 28-30)
Anyone who divorces his wife must give her a certificate of divorce. (verse 31)	Everyone who divorces his wife, makes her commit adultery, except for immorality, and whoever marries a divorced woman commits adultery. (verse 32)
Do not swear falsely but keep the oaths you have made to the Lord. (verse 33)	Do not swear at all; just say "yes" or no." Anything more than this is from evil. (verses 34-37)
An eye for an eye and a tooth for a tooth. (verse 38)	Do not resist the one who is evil, turn the other cheek when struck on the right cheek, give to the one suing or asking or borrowing, and go with the one who forces us. (verses 39-42)
Love your neighbor and hate your enemies. (verse 43)	Love our enemies, pray for those who persecute us, greet those who are not our brothers. (verses 44-47)

From this overview we can see how verses 31-32 are simply one of six parts and each part follows a common structure making up one central message as an organized discourse. Understanding the whole passage is necessary in order for us to comprehend the meaning of the specific example about divorce. Such an understanding prevents us from making the first context mistake—separating this one statement in verses 31-32 from its context.

Together, the bookend verses and the common structure of the in-between "You have heard" commands are strong evidence of a single teaching with an overall, main point, and they indicate that the six comments should be understood and applied consistently.

Now that we have identified the structure of this passage, we are prepared to follow the context. Again, context will help us in two ways:

1. Context will help us come to an understanding of the main purpose of Jesus' sermon in verses 17-48, and

2. Context will help us grasp Jesus' point in verses 31-32 that mention divorce.

As we seek to understand what Jesus is saying in verses 31-32, we will begin by focusing on his main point in the whole passage as he makes his six "You have heard, but I say to you" statements.

The next chapter presents nine questions that will help us identify the main point by first elaborating how our application of the standard interpretation is not consistent with how we apply the other verses in the passage.

2 | Nine Questions That Help Us Understand the Context

This chapter raises nine questions designed to demonstrate how we typically make the first context mistake, i.e., treat Jesus' comment in verses 31-32 differently from his other five comments in the surrounding verses and to challenge the legitimacy of that treatment.

Question 1: What If…?

A typical approach to verses 31-32 is to read them in a literal way leading to the teaching that a person cannot divorce and/or remarry except if the divorce was due to immorality; otherwise, he or she will be an adulterer. Imagine if we Christians applied all Jesus' examples that surround verses 31-32 with the same literal approach we apply to the divorce statement.

If we did apply the other examples with this same literal approach, we would hold a court when someone in our congregation is angry, and we would send to court anyone from our congregation who insulted someone else. We would deal severely with any person who would call someone else a fool since he is guilty of the hell of fire.

Pastors and leaders would teach that when a husband had committed adultery by looking lustfully at a woman, his wife could divorce him, and specific to this "You have heard, but I say to you" statement, the man who had looked lustfully would also be expected to pluck out his eye.

We would not swear any oath or vow, which would include those for jury duty, military service, political office, law enforcement occupations, or weddings. We would not say the American Pledge of Allegiance. We would not vow the Hippocratic Oath or the Pharmacists' Oath; we would not make a vow associated with any professional code of ethics.

We would not resist those who are evil, which would mean we would not resist dangerous individuals who wish to rob, mug, abuse or enslave us. We would always turn the other cheek so it could also be struck.

We would give to everyone who asks something from us,[5] which would include all those standing at the Salvation Army kettles and every missionary or anyone going on any mission trip. It would include the poor or the beggar in the grocery store parking lot and every homeless man or woman holding a sign at a busy intersection. It would include all the mail we get asking for donations to various causes, worthwhile or otherwise. We would truly love every enemy and we would add to our prayer list anyone who persecutes us in any way.

Yet, how many people in our churches have been angry with someone or insulted someone and have been brought before a court? How many sermons have we heard address men who have committed adultery by looking lustfully at a woman, and how many wives have been taught they could divorce their husbands for adultery? How many husbands have plucked out an eye after committing adultery this way? Who has ever plucked out an eye or cut off a hand that has caused sin? The answer to all of these questions is none—none of us practice or enforce these literal consequences! We do not apply these teachings in a literal way.

How many of us have sworn an oath or a vow, ignoring what Jesus very strongly commanded against, and in fact, says is evil? How many of us have not turned the other cheek, ignoring what Jesus instructed? How many of us have resisted or would ever resist an evil person, ignoring what Jesus said? How many of us have been asked to support someone doing missions and not given to him or her, or been asked by a beggar for something and not given to him or her, disregarding what Jesus taught? How many of us know of a time we did not love an enemy or did not pray for someone who persecuted us?

---

[5] In Luke 6:30, Jesus makes it clear by saying, "to *everyone* asking you, give."

We do not apply literal consequences to the examples before verses 31-32, and we do not literally apply what Jesus commanded in the examples after verses 31-32. Since we do not insist the verses before or after must always be applied literally, why do we separate verses 31-32 and treat them differently by insisting we must always apply them in a literal way? Nevertheless, that is what we do, and it demonstrates our faulty exegesis.

We must not be casual with the context, altering the emphasis and changing the application simply to conform Scripture to our own traditions, desires, convenience, or cultural sensibilities.

What is it about verses 31-32 that cause us to apply these verses in such a dramatically different way than every other example in the Matthew 5:17-48 passage?

Chapters 3 and 4 will explain why we do this and will provide a solution so we can be consistent in our application of these verses. But first, we will continue on in our discussion with the next question demonstrating why we should not treat verses 31-32 differently from their surrounding context.

Question 2: Did the Original Audience Apply Literal Consequences?

There is no good reason to assume the original audience applied these examples literally. There is no evidence these people considered they should hold a court when someone was angry. There is no evidence they actually believed a woman would divorce her husband when he became an adulterer by looking lustfully at another woman or any evidence the husband plucked out an eye. There is no evidence in the New Testament of even one person responding "obediently" to Jesus' words by cutting off his own hand.

On the contrary, the Jews continued to utter oaths and vows, they continued to refuse some people who asked from them, they continued to resist some forms of evil.

If Jesus wanted his words in this teaching to be applied literally, we would have to conclude that the Apostles themselves were blatantly disobedient.[6]

Consider that at the time of Jesus, it was the norm in Jewish culture for people to remarry after divorce, and we can assume that some of the people listening to Jesus had been divorced and remarried.[7] Many in that original audience listening to Jesus were devout God-fearers and eager to hear Jesus' teachings because they loved God and wanted to learn how to follow him better. Imagine their consternation if they thought Jesus wanted them to apply these words literally.

For fifteen hundred years, ever since the time of Moses, they would have been committing adultery in this way, including some who were in the crowd listening to Jesus. God-fearers in Jesus' audience, if they had thought Jesus meant to apply his words in verses 31-32 literally, would have been distressed, and expecting further clarification, they would have asked questions such as, "Why didn't Moses tell us this? We never would have done this if we'd known! We want to please God! Why weren't we told? I've remarried after a divorce, what should I do now—divorce again?"

If the crowd had taken Jesus' words literally, many families and relationships would have been turned upside down and many lives ruined. It is almost inconceivable the Bible would not somewhere mention or address the uproar and the ensuing social turmoil that would have arisen if the crowd had understood it should apply a literal meaning to verses 31-32.

---

[6] For example, In 1 Corinthians 4:10, Paul called himself and others "fools," using the same Greek word used in Matthew 5:22. Paul, along with other believers, took vows (Acts 18:18, 21:23-26), and Paul resisted evil (Acts 9:23-25). Peter also resisted evil (Acts 13:8-11). Peter did not cut off his hand when it caused him to sin (John 18:10). We are to say "no" to some people who might ask from us (II Thessalonians 3:10). Paul rebuked the Corinthians because they let themselves be struck in the face (2 Corinthians 11:20). Christians still got angry (Ephesians 4:26).

[7] For more information, see Appendix B: Divorce and Remarriage at the Time of Jesus.

But this is not what we see. We have no indication the crowd understood Jesus to mean that those who had divorced for reasons other than immorality or married a divorced person should now be considered literal adulterers. We see no evidence anywhere in Scripture that people repented or were expected to repent of this adultery. Their reaction, or rather, their lack of a reaction, speaks loudly.[8]

Although we have no record of anyone in the original audience being confused or concerned about remarrying after divorce when they heard Jesus' words in verses 31-32, how helpful it would have been if someone in the crowd had been concerned and would have asked Jesus what he meant.

Thankfully for us, the disciples were concerned about this later and did ask Jesus! What most of us will likely find astonishing is that of all Jesus' "You have heard, but I say to you" statements, the only one he explained was the divorce/remarriage/adultery question. The only one he explained was the one that has caused us the most confusion, and yet, Jesus addressed it specifically to clear up confusion! (We will see this in Part II.)

Since we have no compelling evidence the original audience applied verses 31-32 or the surrounding examples literally, why are we so confident and adamant that we are meant to apply verses 31-32 literally?

Question 3: Why Do We Switch Back and Forth?

What we, the church, seem to have assumed is that Jesus expected his audience not to apply literal consequences to verses 21-30, then abruptly switch and apply literal consequences to verses 31-32, then abruptly switch again and not literally apply verses 33-47.

---

[8] Contrast this with the reaction of Ezra and the Israelites. They correctly took God's rebuke about their marriages to foreign wives literally, and they reacted strongly. See Ezra 9-10, which describe the sin, the prayers of repentance, and the actions taken when the Israelites were confronted with their sinful marriages. This example stands in stark contrast to the lack of serious reaction by Jesus' Jewish audience in Matthew 5:17-48. Jesus' audience knew not to apply this literally.

In order to support such drastic switches in the treatment of verses 31-32, the standard for proof is very high. In other words, the more differently we treat these two verses from the surrounding verses, the stronger the textual justification that is required. A dramatically different understanding of verses 31-32 requires equally dramatic textual indications for its support and defense.

However, there is no textual basis to believe Jesus' followers thought Jesus switched to a literal meaning in verses 31-32. Furthermore, there is no textual basis to believe Jesus changed his method of exposition or his expectations in this way (as we will see in Chapters 3 and 4).

Question 4: Do We Really Want to Live by the Matthew 5 Code?

Despite the questions presented here, some may still want to understand verses 31-32 as a code of rules for Christian conduct. We must be careful! Scripture declares that those who choose to live their lives based on a code cannot break even one single regulation—not even the very least command—they must keep the whole code. If we keep verses 31-32, we must also keep a literal application of the surrounding teachings.

Paul speaks to those who want to live by a code, "I testify again to every man who accepts circumcision that he is obligated to keep the whole law...For all who rely on works of the law are under a curse; for it is written, 'Cursed be everyone who does not abide by *all* things written in the Book of the Law, and do them.'" (Galatians 3:5,10). And James says, "For whoever keeps the whole law but fails in one point has become guilty of *all* of it. For he who said, 'Do not commit adultery, also said, 'Do not murder.' If you do not commit adultery but do murder, you have become a transgressor of the law." (James 2:10).

We should be concerned when we hear this. Why are we not? Paul's and James's words should convince us of the danger, on the one hand, of choosing to literally apply Jesus' words of verses 31-32, but on the other hand, choosing to disregard a literal application of verses 21-30 and 33-47. To those of us who think any of the statements in verses 21-47 should be literally applied, we are warned of the danger of breaking the other commands when it suits us or when it is inconvenient for us to apply them. Their warnings should convince us of the problem of making the Sermon on the Mount into an expanded, improved code of the Old Testament law.

To those who believe Jesus is giving his followers a code of behavior, Scripture teaches that whoever fails in one of the points in verses 21-30 and 33-47 is *also guilty of the adultery of verses 31-32.* We must keep the whole code or we are guilty of all.

Along with this first problem (that we would have to keep every rule of the code), there are additional problems with living by a code. For instance, if we must keep the whole code, how could we possibly be confident we had possession of a complete code? Jesus' illustrations in Matthew 5:17-48 are just that—illustrations. They are not the complete code; for example, Jesus did not illustrate how the people should further fulfill the Sabbath law or pay tithes.

The next problem is even if we were one hundred percent confident we possessed the complete code, we would have to understand the practical application of each rule, but Jesus' illustrations in Matthew 5:17-48 clearly showed that the Jewish leaders and Jewish people were not able to understand the intent or the ramifications or the application of the code, and neither are we. To understand this exceeds human capability.

So then, the problem of living by a code is three-fold. One, we would have to completely understand the practical application of each rule of the code. Two, we would have to keep every single part of the code in all its practical applications without exception. Three, we would have to be confident we possessed the complete code.

Given Scripture's clear warnings about keeping the whole law, what is it about verses 31-32 that make any of us think they are the only rules in this passage we must always apply literally? Chapters 3 and 4 will help us sort this out.

Question 5: Are We Hypocrites?

Next, we will compare the two examples in our passage that mention adultery, verses 27-28 and verses 31-32, and examine inconsistencies in the prevalent understanding and applications of these two examples.

You have heard that it was said, "You shall not commit adultery." But I say to you that everyone who looks at a woman with lustful intent has already committed adultery with her in his heart.[9]
(Matthew5:27-28)

It was also said, "Whoever divorces his wife, let him give her a certificate of divorce." But I say to you that everyone who divorces his wife, except on the ground of sexual immorality, makes her commit adultery, and whoever marries a divorced woman commits adultery.
(Matthew 5:31-32)

Consider:

- Looking at a woman lustfully = Adultery
- Whoever divorces one's spouse = Adultery for that spouse
- Marrying a divorced person = Adultery

Jesus calls all three of these actions adultery. However, the church has very different standards for these adulterers. The first is considered to have little meaning; the second and third are considered to be egregious. The first has minimal consequences; the second and third have burdensome and intrusive consequences.

The church does not call it literal adultery when a man looks at a woman lustfully, does not accept this adultery as justifiable grounds for divorce, and rarely calls men to account who commit this sin. However, the church does call it literal adultery when someone remarries after a divorce not due to immorality, preaching sermons about this sin, often shaming the people who remarry and considering them "second-class Christians" for committing this sin.

---

[9]The word "intent" is not in the Greek text. It could be implied, but it is not found in most translations.

Perhaps we think the disparity in how we treat these two adulteries is justified because Jesus' words "in his heart" mitigate the adultery, or we think it would simply be too hard to prove, or we think looking lustfully is too prevalent, normal, or cannot be helped.

But do the words "in his heart" mitigate the adultery? The Bible does not promote a differentiation like this, but instead, Scripture insists evil comes from the heart and the heart defines who we are,

For out of the heart come evil thoughts, murder, adultery, sexual immorality, theft, false witness, slander. These are what defile a person. But to eat with unwashed hands does not defile anyone. (Matthew 15:19-20)

No. Jesus does not minimize the adultery by saying it happens in the heart; instead, he clarifies the situation by telling us where it takes place. Instead of minimizing the adultery, every Christian should recognize the words "in his heart" as clarifying God's standard and substantiating the reality of the adultery.

This kind of adultery may be hard to prove, but sadly, much of it is very obvious. It is obvious to wives and girlfriends and daughters. It is obvious to male friends. It is obvious by what men look at on the internet and by what they watch on TV, including while watching sporting events or "enjoying" advertisements. It would not be that hard to prove, *if* we decided to apply this adultery as literally as the adultery of verses 31-32.

Possibly the reason we do not apply literal consequences to the adultery when men look lustfully is because we think this sin is so prevalent or considered normal or cannot be helped. Could it be because many of the men in our congregations, including leaders, have committed adultery in this way that we quickly reject the idea of a literal application? Perhaps we assume we are not meant to apply this literally because the result would be widespread guilt and large numbers of divorces.

Nonetheless, neither the prevalence of a sin nor the preponderance of people suffering its consequences should be the determining factor in deciding whether to apply a verse literally. The abundance of Old Testament examples of punishment for widespread sin should convince us that great numbers of guilty people suffering the consequences for their sin does not diminish the reality of the sin or the consequences. Jesus calls it adultery; the fact that it is adultery does not change even if it seems to be a normal reaction or cannot be helped.

The adultery of verses 27-28 should convict almost half the adult population.[10] The majority of men, if they were honest, would have to admit they have looked at a woman lustfully and therefore, have committed adultery. If they would say they have not, it is likely because they have trivialized God's righteous standard by conveniently defining lust to suit themselves—possibly saying something like, "It wasn't real" or "I didn't imagine anything *too* bad!" or "I didn't look or imagine all *that* long" or "I couldn't help it" or any other excusing comment. It is most probable we greatly underestimate God's righteous standard in this area.

If we do not want to be hypocrites, we must apply the same literal consequences to this adultery as we do to the adultery of verses 31-32. The *only* valid reason to reject literal consequences of verses 27-28 is that Jesus did not expect his followers to apply verses 27-28 literally.

It is quite an ingenious teaching method for Jesus to describe this in-the-heart adultery first and make a preemptive statement before he describes the adultery in verses 31-32, before an accusation can be levied against the person described in the adultery of verses 31-32.

Jesus did not make a distinction between these two adulterers. It is Christians who have added the interpretation that the adultery of verses 31-32 is so egregious that remarriage after divorce is forbidden, but the adultery of verses 27-28 is so insignificant as to

---

[10] Jesus may have intended that looking lustfully also applies to women, but he addressed the men.

be inconsequential. By whose authority is this the case? Certainly not by Jesus' authority. Jesus gives no indication the adultery of verses 31-32 should be interpreted and applied differently or given worse consequences. If anything, the adultery of verses 27-28 should be considered much worse because in his next words, Jesus says the man should pluck out his eye!

It is hypocrisy when we forbid people to marry based on verses 31-32, while at the same time we disregard consequences for men who, according to verses 27-28, become adulterers by looking lustfully at women. We should insist verses 31-32 are no more to be applied literally than verses 27-28.

Question 6: Remarrying after Divorce Is the Worst Sin, Right?

There are some churches that will not allow people to hold certain leadership positions, work in certain ministries, or even become official members of their congregation if they have divorced and remarried. They expect the remarried to first repent of committing adultery, and even then, many churches and Christian organizations limit these people to what are considered less meaningful jobs. The divorced are often considered second-class Christians in our churches and Christian organizations, and it is worse for those who have remarried after divorce. Even some church members that will not openly look down on the divorced and remarried privately condemn them.

These churches and organizations and many of us Christians treat the divorced as somehow less mature or less spiritual than the ones who have not divorced, and we treat them this way even as we ourselves break Jesus' other "but I say to you" statements in Matthew 5:17-48.

There is no indication by Jesus that a divorce would make someone less mature or less spiritual than disregarding any other of the Matthew 5:17-48 statements, than for example, swearing an oath or not giving to someone who asked or looking at a woman lustfully.

To see this more clearly, consider Jesus says the following:

With regard to calling someone a fool—

- This person is guilty of *the hell of fire*.

With regard to looking at a woman lustfully—

- It is adultery.
- The man should *pluck out his eye*.

With regard to swearing an oath—

- Do not swear.
- At all.
- Let your "yes" be "yes" and your "no" "no."
- Anything more than this *is from evil*.

A good argument could be made that these three are much worse than the adultery of verses 31-32 because for these three, besides mentioning the sin, Jesus includes *additional* consequences and warnings.

Is there any good reason to separate verses 31-32 from the rest of Matthew 5:17-48 as somehow different, as somehow more egregious? Why assume that is the only item in Matthew 5:17-48 that is worth making people repent of before they join a church or serve in a church? Is this worse than anything else listed in Matthew 5:17-48? If we think it is worse, why do we think it is? And what are the criteria we use to determine our list of "Items in Matthew 5 that Are Okay to Neglect" and "Items in Matthew 5 that Are So Egregious They Are Worthy of Demotion to Second-Class Christian"? We have no biblical grounds to make these distinctions.

Question 7: But the Divorce Consequence Is Easy to Apply, So Why Wouldn't We?

Some might make the argument that verses 31-32 should be treated differently because they seem to be easy to apply—"Just don't get married after a divorce!" This response misses the main point Jesus is making in the larger passage, but setting this misunderstanding aside, the response itself simply does not stand— we will soon see that Jesus and Paul both reject this thinking.

In Part II and in Part IV, we will examine this argument and will see that both Jesus and Paul have an answer for those people who would say, "Just don't get married after a divorce."

Question 8: Oh No! Will This Open the Floodgates?

There are those of us who will say, "I understand the argument, but if we were to stop teaching an Exception Clause, there will be even more divorces in the church than there are now." This thinking reflects a concern that if we stop applying literal consequences to verses 31-32, we will "open the floodgates." It reflects a desire to protect marriage and a belief that any softening of the stance will weaken marriage and result in more and more divorces in the church. It concludes that since we do not want to be responsible in any way for more divorce, we will keep applying verses 31-32 always in a literal way.

Are we confident the church would be better off if we applied literal consequences to verses 31-32 even if it was not Jesus' intention? It is a worthy goal to want to minimize divorce, but it must be done within Scriptural parameters. When we try to minimize divorce by applying verses 31-32 literally, we have at least two problems.

First, the church may think it is doing a good thing if it adds to or subtracts from Scripture to help people become "more righteous," but this is not the church's prerogative. This attitude, in effect, declares we know better than God how to equip the church and to bring it to sanctification. The church should not rely on extraneous rules to prevent sin or to stop the floodgates from opening. We who have been born again and are new creations should rely on the leading of the Holy Spirit and the transforming power of the Word of God to equip and to guide and to discern and to prevent sin. Adding rules to prevent sin is the vocation of Pharisees. [11]

Second, following extra-biblical rules to prevent divorce allows a church to pretend the couples in the church have good

---

[11] The Pharisees will be discussed several times in this book. See Appendix C for an overview about them.

marriages, or even better marriages than the world, even the marriages that are so bad they might be considered to be shams. In some churches there are almost the same number of divorces as in the world. Perhaps the divorce rate is lower in the church you attend. The question is, does a lower divorce rate in a church reflect healthy marriages? Or does it simply reflect the church's pressure on couples to remain married? If the latter, that is not something to consider as a positive.

If we accurately teach what God's word says and means, we might possibly have more divorces in the church. Yes, this is a solemn and important issue. But the greater concern here is that we might presume to think we have the wisdom to know better than Jesus what to teach. Anyone who knows Scripture means A, but then teaches B, seems to be pushing God out of the way (to put it mildly). We might have good intentions, but every motive must be subservient to rightly dividing the Word of Truth.

In Part II, we will further discuss whether it is better to forbid remarriage after divorce.

Question 9: Who Decides?

We have discussed that applying verses 31-32 in a literal way is a major departure from how we apply the rest of Jesus' examples. A second major departure is found in who decides the application of these examples. For instance, who decides which examples to apply literally? Who decides if someone has kept or broken one of the Matthew 5 commands? Who decides if someone must repent publicly? Who decides if a person can repent privately? Who decides if a person needs to repent at all?

To be specific, who decides if a person is angry or has insulted someone or if his hand has caused him to sin or if he has refused to give to someone who asked or if he is allowed to swear an oath? Who decides if someone has an enemy? Who decides what the love we show an enemy looks like? Who decides if we need to make things right? Is it the individual himself? Is it church leaders? A pastor somewhere?

Who decides if a man has looked at a woman lustfully? Who determines the definition of that lust? Who determines the definition of sexual immorality? Who decides when someone has crossed the line and has become sexually immoral? Is it the immoral man himself who decides? His wife? His girlfriend? Church leaders?

At the end of the Sermon on the Mount, we read, "The result was that when Jesus had finished these words, the multitudes were amazed at his teaching, for he was teaching them as having authority and not as the scribes" (Matthew 7:28-29). Before Jesus came, the Jewish people were trapped and held in bondage by the rules and decisions of the Pharisees and the other religious leaders of the day. These leaders were the adjudicators and the final authority of how and when to keep the laws, and they were the determiners of righteousness.

Speaking by his own authority, Jesus challenged the established leaders and stripped from them the authority they had wrongfully usurped. For followers of Jesus, these established leaders would no longer be the ones to define behavior or righteousness. Jesus freed the crowds, and us, from this darkness and bondage to human rules and human decree.

But then, to whom did Jesus give the power to decide these things? Excluding verses 31-32, when it comes to Jesus' other Matthew 5 examples, we expect each believer will rely on the Holy Spirit's guidance to decide if, when, how, to what extent, or in what circumstances he or she will apply any of these examples. This works well as the church rightly thinks the individual believer is the one who should make his or her behavioral decisions as guided by Scripture and the leading of the Holy Spirit. Jesus said as he prayed to the Father, "Sanctify them in the truth. Your Word is truth" (John 17:17). And Paul says, "Walk by the Spirit and you will not fulfill the desires of the flesh" (Galatians 5:16).

Of course, some flagrant sins and sins that impact the church might need to be dealt with by the church, but for the most part, each individual believer determines his or her own life choices and behaviors. This decision-making and leading through the Word and the Holy Spirit is called discernment. Those who are given, or rather, those who *use* spiritual discernment do not need lists of rules.

When it comes to all the other issues in Matthew 5:17-48, we each make our own decisions about behavior, whether to apply Jesus' examples in a literal way and when or how to apply them, but when it comes to the divorce verses, in many of our local fellowships and congregations, everything changes abruptly.

Too often, when a couple contemplates divorcing, they suddenly lose their own decision-making capabilities and privileges, at least that is the practical result as far as the couple is concerned. From all corners come Christians, even people they barely know, with the purpose of imposing their will on the couple, to tell them what they should do or not do and whether they have biblical authority to divorce or not, or to remarry or not. Church leaders call them in to reprimand and dictate to them, attempting to stop a divorce or warning that he or she will not be able to remarry.

How has it happened that in this matter we have ceded our discernment and decision-making privilege to others? How has it happened that when it comes to divorce, Christians who were previously allowed to discern God's will for their own lives and considered capable of doing so, now, in the eyes of the church, suddenly become incapable?

How has it happened that others decide if and when and under what circumstances a believer can divorce and if and when and under what circumstances a believer can remarry? Chapters 3 and 4 will give us some answers.

To summarize this chapter, those of us who care about and understand the importance of context and expositional teaching must agree that if verses 31-32 are intended to be applied literally, then the other five "You have heard, but I say to you" statements are intended to be applied literally. Conversely, if the other five are *not* intended to be applied literally, then verses 31-32 (without some strong and clear textual indication otherwise) are also *not* intended to be applied literally—all six must be treated consistently and even-handedly across the board.

3 | Going Down the Wrong Path

Jesus did not implicitly or explicitly communicate to us that he made a change in the context in his sermon at Matthew 5:31-32. Nevertheless, for decades of church history, Christians have made an abrupt switch in interpretation when we read these verses. We apply these verses in a literal way, which is inconsistent with how we apply the rest of Matthew 5:17-48. Why would we do this?

What is it about Matthew 5:31-32 that causes us abruptly to switch our approach, to change the context, and to hear Jesus' speak in such a different style and tone than the rest of the passage? What is it that seems to indicate such a change that we are willing to apply these verses so much more literally than the rest of the passage? This departure from the style and context of the rest of the sermon should make every Christian sit up and ask, "What happened here? Did Jesus change his teaching style for just these two verses?"

These are good questions, rarely asked questions, and even more, they are rarely answered questions, which is too bad because the answer is entirely too critical to miss.

What *Parektos* Teaches Us

The answer is Jesus did not change his tone or style. *It is translators and teachers that change the tone and style by their choice of one simple word*—"except."

A typical translation uses the word "except,"

*But I say to you that everyone who divorces his wife, **except** on the ground of sexual immorality, makes her commit adultery, and whoever marries a divorced woman commits adultery.*

The "except" phrase makes us think that Jesus is giving his followers a rule for living the Christian life. It is this "Exception

Clause" that has us thinking these two verses should be applied literally.

"Except" here is key, but is the original word really "except?"

When Matthew wrote verse 32, he did not use the Greek words that are usually translated "except." The Greek *ei mē* or *ean mē* have the meaning "except" and appear over one hundred times in the Greek New Testament—we would expect to see these words in verse 32 of the Greek text.

However, neither of these frequently used Greek words are what Matthew recorded in verse 32. Instead, Matthew used a different Greek word, and a rarely used word at that. Matthew used a word found only three times in the Greek New Testament—a word that has profound implications for the divorce discussion. The Greek word Matthew used is *parektos* (as mentioned in Chapter 1, the three-word clause is *parektos logou porneias*).[12]

Why did Matthew use *parektos* in this verse and not *ei mē* or *ean mē*? A curious and aware student reading this word would say, "I don't know this word. I should look into it and investigate further. How can I understand the divorce verses or this passage if I don't know this word?"

We should care about the answer to this question. It should lead to deliberation and discussion. It should drive us to our lexicons to find a definition that fits the context and satisfies our questions.

Definition of *Parektos*

The definitions from the Greek lexicon for *parektos* are "besides," "outside," "apart from," and "except for."[13]

---

[12] See Appendix A for more discussion of *ei mē*, *ean mē*, *parektos*, and the other two uses of *parektos*.

[13] Walter Bauer, *A Greek-English Lexicon of the New Testament and Other Early Christian Literature, 3rd ed.* Revised and Edited by Frederick William Danker. (BDAG) (Chicago: The University of Chicago Press, 2000), 774

It is true the English "except for" is one of the Greek lexicon's definitions for *parektos*, but "except for" and "except" do not convey the same idea.[14] While both are prepositions that mean "not including" or "excluding," there is a basic and crucial difference between the two. When "except for" is used in a phrase, the phrase is de-emphasized, but when "except" is used in a phrase, the phrase is emphasized.

For English speakers, hearing or reading the word "except" in a sentence influences our understanding of the meaning of what we hear or read. It is the nature of the English language that the word "except" when used in a sentence *causes us to focus on the except phrase;* the except phrase is emphasized.[15] This placement of emphasis can be subtle; we are often unaware when our focus shifts. The normal reaction for English speakers when hearing or reading the word "except" in a sentence is to emphasize the clause, but such an emphasis is not appropriate when *parektos* is used, as in our verse.

Parektos Does Not Emphasize a Phrase

Erroneously using "except" in verse 32 causes most English speakers to emphasize a phrase that should not be emphasized. The more appropriate way to think of this *parektos* clause is as a "besides" clause. A "besides" clause is like a parenthetical phrase, minimizing its importance. In fact, William Tyndale, whose translation was the first English Bible that drew directly from Greek and Hebrew texts, actually put this phrase in parentheses, thereby showing he understood that in the Greek, this phrase is meant to be de-emphasized.[16]

---

[14] Many English speakers are unaware of the difference between the two. A glimpse of some of the discussion can be seen at this website: http://eltj.oxfordjournals.org/content/XXXV/3/260.extract

[15] *Webster's New Universal Unabridged Dictionary* (New York: Barnes & Noble Books, 1996), s.v. "except," 674

[16] William Tyndale, *The New Testament: The text of the Worms edition of 1526 in original spelling,* ed. W.R. Cooper (London: The British Library, 2000), 11. Also, William Tyndale, *The New Testament: A Reprint of the Edition of 1534 with the Translator's Prefaces & Notes and the variants of the edition of 1525,* ed. N. Hardy Wallis (London, Cambridge University Press, 1938), 32

The primary meaning is more accurately conveyed if we read the verse with the clause in parentheses,

Everyone who divorces his wife (besides for immorality) makes her to commit adultery, and whoever marries a divorced woman commits adultery.

Here is a key point—when first century Christians read the word *parektos* in verse 32, they would have understood the idea of "besides," "apart from," or "outside" and de-emphasized the phrase. Accordingly, our English usage must denote this meaning. Only then we will be able to grasp the point of verses 31-32, and only then we will be able to keep verses 31-32 in context.

It is when we do not understand the accurate meaning of *parektos* that we are inclined to read and apply these verses differently than the rest of Jesus' "You have heard, but I say to you" statements.

To guard against this error

- we must know *parektos* is the word used in verse 32.
- we must understand the definition of *parektos.*
- our words and translation must agree with this definition.

An accurate meaning for *parektos* will keep verses 31-32 in context.

We will use the following example to illustrate what the use of the word "besides" conveys (and does not convey). It will help us see what Jesus meant by his "besides" clause (and what he did not mean) and why the clause was necessary to help the Jews understand Jesus' point.

A Helpful Example

Suppose a "Professor Taylor" had said the following to his students,

"You've heard that there will be a comprehensive final in this class. I tell you there are ways to prepare for it (besides review sessions) such as rereading the material and doing extra homework pages."

The following 5 comments use this example to help us get a more accurate understanding of what Jesus meant by his *parektos* clause, his "besides" clause.

Comment 1

From reading Professor Taylor's "besides clause," can you tell what Professor Taylor thinks about review sessions? Does he usually have them? Never have them? Is he planning to have one? Not planning to have one? Does he think they're helpful? Does he dislike them?

In fact, none of these questions can be answered from the information in that short, three-word "besides" clause; the information is insufficient to answer those questions. We do not know what Professor Taylor thinks about review sessions from that clause.

To further explain, we will tell you that Professor Taylor *never* has review sessions. However, "Professor Carson," a colleague, *always* has review sessions.

Whether a professor *never* has review sessions or *always* has review sessions, either professor could say to his class, "You've heard that there will be a comprehensive final in this class. I tell you there are ways to prepare for it (besides review sessions) such as rereading the material and doing extra homework pages." Professor Taylor, who is not going to have a review session, could say this, and Professor Carson, who is going to have a review session, could say this.

This very important illustration should reinforce the conclusion above that the three-word besides clause does not provide information about either professor's position about review sessions. That *both* professors can make a "besides statement" shows us the clause itself conveys no information about their preferences regarding review sessions.

It would be going too far for anyone to say he or she knows what Professor Taylor thinks about review sessions from his "besides review sessions" statement by itself.

Likewise, Jesus could have added his three-word *parektos* clause regardless of whether he was against allowing divorce for *porneia*, for it, sometimes for/against it, or if in fact, he added the clause for some other reason, which is the view of this book. This uncertainty is one reason why it is going too far to say we know Jesus' position about divorce for *porneia* from his three-word *parektos* clause.

Comment 2

Since what Professor Taylor thinks about review sessions cannot be determined from his besides clause, the only way we can find out his position about review sessions would be to ask him or find out what he said somewhere else about review sessions.

Likewise, since Jesus' position about divorce for *porneia* cannot be determined from his *parektos* clause, the only way we can find out would be to ask him or look elsewhere at other statements Jesus made about this topic. However, Jesus makes only one other divorce statement with a *porneia* clause, and it is similar to this one. We cannot know from that clause either (Matthew 19:9, discussed in Part II).

Comment 3

From the "besides" clause alone, we cannot know either Professor Taylor's or Professor Carson's opinion about review sessions—*but that does not matter because neither is making a point about review sessions*; both professors want the students to focus on the two methods (rereading and extra homework). Both professors are directing students' attention to *the two methods*.

Similarly, from Jesus' *parektos* clause, we cannot know his position on divorce for *porneia*—*but it does not matter because that is not his point*. Jesus wants the focus or emphasis to be on the message conveyed by the rest of his sentence.

Jesus wants his listeners to focus on a reality about divorce, remarriage, and adultery. This *true, comprehensive reality* is what Jesus wants his listeners to know, and this reality is conveyed in the rest of Jesus' sentence.

Comment 4

Professor Taylor does not want his students to sit around and focus on the "besides" clause. Professor Taylor is saying to his students, "Look here (at rereading the material and doing extra homework pages). Don't look there (at review sessions)!"

In fact, Professor Taylor does not even regard review sessions as a way to study for the final; he mentions them *but then he sets them aside* (he de-emphasizes them). When he lists the two ways to study, he is not saying these two are *other* ways to study *in addition* to review sessions. No. Professor Taylor wants the students to use the two ways, and he is *not* including review sessions.

Similarly, Jesus does not want his listeners to sit around and focus on the *parektos* clause. Jesus is saying, "Don't look there (at the *parektos* clause). Look here at the rest of my sentence to learn the reality about divorce, remarriage, and adultery!"

And just as Professor Taylor wanted the students to exclude review sessions from their study plans, Jesus wanted his audience to exclude their understanding about divorce-due-to-immorality because their view about that situation might color how they interpreted the truth revealed in the rest of his statement. Jesus conveys the true reality in the rest of his statement, and he does not want that reality interpreted in light of what they thought they knew about divorce.

Comment 5

This is where the practical application comes in. Misunderstanding and misapplying the *parektos* clause can result in grave, unintended consequences. If we (the church) misunderstand and think that Jesus meant he allows divorce for adultery (adultery is the typical example used for *porneia*), then we must tell all the couples who have this issue—100% of them—that Jesus allows them to divorce for the adultery; this would be the forthright and honest approach. However, if we do this, we might be giving the go ahead for divorce to many couples that God would not have given.

Suppose, hypothetically, that God would give only 20% of couples with this issue the go ahead to divorce and God would want the remaining 80% to stay together and work through it. Then in this example, the church's presumption that the *parektos* clause gives the go ahead for divorce for adultery would mean that the church would be giving many more couples the green light to divorce than God would have given! The church would be responsible for the dissolution of many, many marriages that God intended to stay together.

Because God knows the hearts of the people in marriages where adultery has occurred, God alone would know who would be able to get past this and keep their marriage together.

Why Did Jesus Include the *Parektos* Clause?

To help explain why Jesus included the *parektos* clause, we will first tell you why Professor Taylor does not have review sessions. Professor Taylor has found that many of his students have a serious misconception about review sessions. They mistakenly believe that the questions and answers discussed in a one or two-hour review session will be enough information to prepare for the final. They have a false confidence that once they understand the topics covered in the review session, they will be prepared for the final; they have a false confidence that is all they need to know. This misconception causes students to miss the true and complete understanding of how best to learn the material and prepare for the final, and it causes them to miss their true situation—that their grasp of how to study for the final is shallow.

Likewise, Jesus included his *parektos* clause for similar reasons. The Jews had a misconception about adultery and divorce, and their confidence in that misconception caused them to miss God's reality. They had a shallow grasp of the issue, and this caused them to miss the magnitude of God's holiness.

Traditionally the Jewish response in cases of adultery was to divorce—historical records tell us the Jews understood that immorality would lead to divorce. David Instone-Brewer says, "Divorce for immorality was not compulsory, but it was generally assumed that a husband would want to divorce an unfaithful wife."[17] Also, consider Joseph, who, because he thought Mary had committed adultery, had in mind to divorce her (Matthew 1:19). The Jews were quite confident in this understanding about divorce; their understanding made sound, moral sense to them.

However, it is likely that *it was this very confidence that would cause them to miss the reality of God's truth*; that is, God's perspective, which as humans, they had missed. Thus, setting aside their existing understanding with the *parektos* clause was necessary. With no *parektos* clause, the Jews likely would have taken Jesus' statement the wrong way and thought something along the lines of, "We know what you mean. You are talking about divorce when there is adultery—when *those who have committed adultery* remarry, *they* are still adulterers."

In fact, Jesus did not even give them a chance to take it the wrong way. Theirs was a shallow understanding of the true reality of the situation, and with the *parektos* clause, Jesus recognized *and then set aside* their limited understanding about divorce. Indeed, Jesus brings up the *parektos* clause—not because it was his view about divorce—but because it stated the Jews' view, their understanding. Their "mental rut" would have kept them from

---

[17] David Instone-Brewer, *Divorce and Remarriage in the Bible* (Grand Rapids: William B. Eerdmans Publishing Company, 2002), 97. For his fuller discussion of the history of divorce for adultery, see pages 94-99.

seeing the truth Jesus was communicating, but they were able to get out of their rut and hear the true situation with the help of the *parektos* clause (which set aside their shallow understanding).

It was the Jews' overconfidence in their position about divorce that would have kept them from seeing the big picture and the reality of how God views divorce, remarriage, and adultery.

The purpose of the *parektos* clause is to direct listeners away from their own view of divorce for adultery and direct them to the truth and the reality of the situation.

What Is the Reality of God's Truth?

If we de-emphasize the *parektos* phrase, if we put it aside for a minute, then we can properly focus on the statement Jesus meant to be his point. This is found in the "but I say to you" part of his statement,

Anyone who divorces his wife makes her commit adultery, and whoever marries a divorced woman commits adultery.

Remember that for Jews in the first century, remarriage after divorce was the cultural norm; it was expected that the divorced would likely remarry.[18] Therefore, when Jesus says, "...makes her commit adultery," he means that it is when she remarries that she commits adultery.

Notice first in this verse that Jesus is not giving guidelines about when divorce is allowed. He is stating something about marriage—marriage by divorced persons and marriage to divorced persons.

Second, divorce makes the woman commit adultery (because of the unstated assumption that a divorced woman will remarry). Given this assumption, the statement says every woman who is divorced and marries again commits adultery. No conditions or

---

[18] See Appendix B, Divorce and Remarriage at the Time of Jesus.

exceptions are given. (This would also be the case if the husband is divorced and marries again.)

Third, Jesus' statement says *whoever* marries a divorced person commits adultery. This includes those whose first marriage is to a divorced person—one who has never been married before will commit adultery by marrying a divorced person.

A Few Brief Examples

The following examples help explain Jesus' statement:

1) Consider "Mr. B" and his ex-wife who are divorced because he committed adultery. Even if his ex-wife is what we call "the innocent party" (the one whose husband committed adultery against her), she commits adultery when she marries again merely because she has been *divorced*. Every person who remarries after a divorce commits adultery, no matter what the cause of the divorce, no matter if that person is "the innocent party."

2) Suppose Mr. B who is divorced because he committed adultery remarries, and when he remarries, he marries a virgin. According to Jesus, this virgin woman becomes an adulterer because she married Mr. B who is a *divorced* person (*not* because she married Mr. B who was an adulterer).

3) In fact, if the virgin woman married a different man, a Mr. R who was divorced for a reason *other than porneia/adultery*, the virgin woman would still become an adulterer when she married simply because the man she married was *divorced*, and his reason for being divorced does not make a difference.

4) In addition, Mr. R, who was divorced but had never committed adultery, would become an adulterer when he remarried simply because he was a *divorced* person who remarried.

The Jews had a shallow understanding about the seriousness of adultery and divorce, and Jesus' statement was meant to point that out. Jesus' point is that *all* marriage by a divorced person or to a divorced person is adultery. This is the true reality he is communicating. The situation is much, much more serious than the Jews had thought. God's standard of holiness is so much higher than any of us have ever thought.

Is Divorce Part of Your Life Experience? Do Not Despair!

Right now, someone may be thinking, "But my husband committed adultery against me, and my pastor said I could remarry after my divorce. He said I would not be an adulterer if I remarried, so I remarried. Now you say I'm an adulterer!"

Your pastor mistakenly thought the verse had an Exception Clause when he gave his advice. There is no Exception Clause. No exceptions are stated here.

But do not despair! Although Jesus says the people in these situations commit adultery, he had a purpose for saying this, which we will discuss in the next chapter. We will soon see the reason this discussion is important. Context! We do not want to make the first context mistake. We must treat this "You have heard, but I say to you" statement in the same way we treat the rest of Jesus' "You have heard, but I say to you" statements.

"Besides" Puts Verses 31-32 in Context

When we read verses 31-32 with the *parektos* idea of "besides," we find that the verses are entirely in context with the rest of Matthew 5:21-47. We see the flow of the context does not change and that Jesus did not make "switches" as he spoke.

Perhaps you have not yet realized Jesus' point in Matthew 5:17-48 or have a hard time seeing why *parektos* keeps verses 31-32 entirely in the context of Matthew 5:21-47. And more importantly, perhaps at this point you are thinking that with no Exception Clause, Jesus is teaching a stricter situation than we had ever thought—that *all* marriage by a divorced person or to a divorced person is adultery.

Could this more accurate reading of Matthew 5:31-32 make verses 31-32 fit the context? Could this more accurate reading change our thinking about remarrying after divorce? Is it possible a correct understanding of *parektos* can help us grasp Jesus' point and purpose in Matthew 5:17-48?

The answer to these questions is yes, and if you are wondering how it will help us understand Jesus' point, read on. Chapter 4 will make this clear.

4 | It's a Salvation Message!

Two Choices

An understanding of *parektos* helps us read Jesus' statement in Matthew 5:31-32 accurately, that all marrying by or to divorced persons is adultery. No exceptions are given. There is no "Exception Clause."

The statement "All marrying by or to a divorced person is adultery" forces us to make a choice. Does Jesus, in fact, actually mean that no divorced person can ever marry and no one can ever marry a divorced person because he or she would then commit adultery? Does Jesus want us to live this way? Or does he have another purpose in saying this?

Up until now, most of us have believed there are circumstances when remarriage after divorce is allowed, and it seems Scripture indicates this. With our new reading of Jesus' words, we have to choose between two options. The first option is to say we were wrong before when we allowed remarriage under certain circumstances, and the rule is now "No marriage by a divorced person or to a divorced person is ever allowed."

The second option is to conclude Jesus is not giving divorce or remarriage rules, but that he wants us to hear something else—to conclude he had a different purpose behind the divorce verses, a different purpose behind all the "You have heard, but I say to you" statements other than to provide literal rules for behavior.

Let us look at a summary chart comparing what Jesus said with what his statements would mean if they were applied literally.

If We Applied Jesus' Words Literally

Jesus Said...	If It Is literal, It Means...
Whoever is angry with his brother is also liable to the judgment, whoever insults his brother will be liable to the council, whoever says, "you fool!" will be liable to the hell of fire. (verses 22-26)	We must never get angry with or insult our brother or we face judgment or a court. We must never call someone a fool or we are guilty of the hell of fire.
If a man looks lustfully at a woman, he has committed adultery with her in his heart, if our right eye causes us to sin, we should tear it out, and if our right hand causes us to sin, we should cut it off. (verses 28-30)	A man must never look at a woman lustfully; if he does, he commits adultery. When our eye or hand causes us to sin, we must pluck out the eye or cut off the hand.
Everyone who divorces his wife makes her commit adultery, and whoever marries a divorced woman commits adultery. (verse 32)	We must never remarry after a divorce, and we must never marry a divorced person; if we do, we commit adultery.
Do not swear at all. Just say "yes" or "no." Anything more than this is from evil. Verses 34-37)	We must never swear any oath; if we do, we participate with evil.
Do not resist the one who is evil. Turn the other cheek if someone strikes the right cheek. Give to the one suing, asking, or borrowing. Go with the one who forces us. (verses 39-42)	We must not resist an evil person. We must always turn the other cheek. We must give to the one suing, asking, or borrowing. We must always go with the one forcing us.

If We Applied Jesus' Words Literally, continued

Jesus Said...	If It Is literal, It Means...
Love our enemies. Pray for those who persecute us. Greet those who are not our brothers. (verses 44-47)	We must love every enemy. We must pray for everyone who persecutes us. We must greet everyone who is not our brother.

Literal applications of Jesus' Matthew 5 examples would be extreme in most circumstances, impossible for at least two of them, a hardship in some, and impractical in others. Most are not clear as to when they should be applied, and some leave us with more questions than they answer. For example, "What exactly is 'looking lustfully'?" "How angry does one have to be to be considered angry?" "Is using a word like 'stupid' or 'dummy' or 'moron' the same as calling someone a fool?"[19] "Does *any* name calling make me guilty of the fire of hell, and does this mean I lose my salvation?" "Am I guilty if I don't give to those who ask but who refuse to work?" "Am I guilty if I've tried to love my enemy but still don't?" "Am I guilty if I 'pledge allegiance to a flag'? Is that an oath?"

Even our pastors do not agree. One pastor will say, "This verse is to be applied in our relationships with believers and this other one is to be applied in our relationships with nonbelievers; this one is to be applied only when we individually face a certain situation and this other is to be applied when the church faces the situation." Yet another pastor will say the opposite. Other pastors simply ignore some, for example, cutting off a hand or guilty of the fire of hell.

As for Matthew 5:31-32, wrongly thinking it contains an Exception Clause, one pastor will say, "You can divorce only if your spouse committed adultery," and another will say, "You can remarry only if your spouse committed adultery," while another will say,

---

[19] The Greek transliterates as *moron*.

"You can remarry only if your spouse committed adultery *or* was abusive (some will add, "only if the wife's life is in danger"), and yet another will say, "Jesus meant divorce is allowed only during the engagement period and only if there is immorality during the engagement period."

If Jesus' "but I say to you" statements in Matthew 5:17-48 are meant to be applied literally, we find ourselves at a loss as to when and in what circumstances to apply them. Over and over, we find ourselves applying them inconsistently or only when convenient. Matthew 5:17-48 might be the most arbitrarily and inconsistently applied passage in Scripture.

But could there be one way to look at these that will be consistent and not arbitrary? Yes, there is a way to understand this passage other than as providing a list of behavioral rules for living as a Christian, but we need to consider Jesus' purpose for the entire Matthew 5:17-48 passage.

To Whom Is Jesus Speaking?

In Matthew 5:17-48, Jesus was specifically talking to crowds of enthusiastic followers (Matthew 4:25, 5:1, 8:1). They were the ones who heard him gladly (Mark 12:37, Luke 13:17), they were the ones who got up early to hear him (Luke 21:38), and they were the crowds that stayed with him for days (Matthew 14:13-21). They were the crowds who were amazed at his teaching because he taught with authority, not as their teachers of the law (Matthew 7:28-29). These people thought well of Jesus to the extent they thought he might be one of the prophets of old or even the promised Messiah (John 7:40-41). They were God fearers. They were people who knew the law and wanted to please God by keeping it.

We see this in Jesus' use of the second person throughout Matthew 5:17-48. Jesus addresses the crowds as believers in and sincere followers of the true God, "*You* are the salt of the earth," "*You* are the light of the world," "Let *your* light shine before others so that they may see *your* good works and give glory to *your Father* who is in heaven."[20]

Many in this crowd were likely blameless or devout in their keeping of the law (Luke 1:6, Acts 22:12). Jesus' sermon with its "You have heard" statements specifically addressed the law and was directed toward those who desired to please God and who cared about keeping the law.[21]

It is also important to recognize the two groups to whom Jesus *was not* speaking in this passage. First, Jesus was not speaking to Pharisees, and those like the Pharisees, who thought they were already righteous before God and who were not interested in being taught how they might better understand and follow God's ways. In this passage, Jesus spoke about the Pharisees, but not to them. This is seen when he told the crowd, "Unless your righteousness surpasses the righteousness of the Scribes and Pharisees, you will not enter the kingdom of Heaven." For their part, the Pharisees did not think of Jesus as *their* teacher (Matthew 9:11). Instead of gladly hearing him, they scoffed at him (Luke 16:14), and in fact, many times, Scripture demonstrates they were clearly antagonists.

Second, Jesus was not speaking to those who did not acknowledge God or to those who had no interest in being righteous before God or who were embracing a sinful lifestyle. These people, of course, were not interested in learning from Jesus.

Our Reality vs. God's Standard

Recognizing that Jesus is speaking to sincere believers and followers of the true God, let us consider the "bookend" verses.

---

[20] When the Greek New Testament uses the second person ("you"), it means the person or persons (or class of persons) being addressed. Second person does not mean people in general as it sometimes does in English.

[21] We should not be surprised, but should have expected that when Jesus came, he would address questions about the Law, and he does this in Matthew 5:17-48.

Jesus began the Matthew 5:17-48 passage by saying,

Do not think that I have come to abolish the Law or the Prophets; I have not come to abolish them but to fulfill them. For truly, I say to you, until heaven and earth pass away, not an iota, not a dot, will pass from the Law until all is accomplished. Therefore whoever relaxes one of the least of these commandments and teaches others to do the same will be called least in the kingdom of heaven, but whoever does them and teaches them will be called great in the kingdom of heaven. For I tell you, unless your righteousness exceeds that of the scribes and Pharisees, you will never enter the kingdom of heaven.   (Matthew 5:17-20)

And Jesus ended by saying,

You therefore must be perfect, as your heavenly Father is perfect.   (Matthew 7:48)

Our righteousness must exceed that of the scribes and Pharisees, and we must be perfect. What are we to make of this?

Most of the people listening to Jesus loved God and wanted to be obedient, and they were devout in their keeping of the law. Indeed, the first part of Jesus' "You have heard, but I say to you" statements is a command from the Old Testament law, and each is a command that these devout Jews in the crowd fulfilled.

Consider:

1. *Do not murder and anyone who murders will be liable to the judgment.*

   These Jews listening to Jesus did not murder, and they brought murderers to judgment.

2. *Do not commit adultery.*

   These devout Jews did not commit adultery.

3. *Anyone who divorces his wife must give her a certificate of divorce.*

    When the Jews divorced, they followed Moses' command to give a certificate of divorce.

4. *Do not swear falsely.*

    These devout Jews listening to Jesus did not swear falsely; they kept their word.

5. *An eye for an eye and a tooth for a tooth.*

    The Jews kept this Old Testament command; they gave out justice fairly.

6. *Love your neighbor and hate your enemies.*

    The Jews practiced love for their neighbors.

The Jews in the crowd loved God, and we should consider them, at least the majority of them, blameless and devout in their keeping of the law. Jesus does not condemn them in their keeping of the "You have heard" part of his statement.

Nevertheless, the second part of Jesus' statements, the "but I say to you" part, shows how far even sincere followers actually were from understanding, attaining, and satisfying God's holy standard. Each of Jesus' "but I say to you" statements demonstrates that although these Jews might love God and keep the law, in truth, they had not grasped how impossible it is to truly satisfy God's holiness. Jesus' words demonstrate they fell far short of God's standard of holiness.

Think of it—guilty of the fiery hell for merely calling someone a fool, guilty of adultery for looking at a woman lustfully, plucking out an eye or cutting off a hand when it causes sin, being a participant with evil by swearing an oath, not resisting an evil person—all these are extreme. And a correct understanding of the *parektos* clause also puts verses 31-32 in the same extreme category as the other five "but I say to you" statements—that all marriage by a divorced person or to a divorced person is adultery.

All these statements, *every one of them*, are on a level that is beyond our earthly, human ability to satisfy.

Given this new understanding, we see that Matthew 5:31-32 fits the context of Matthew 5:17-48.

Compare:

> In the other five "You have heard, but I say to you" statements, Jesus
>
> - first states an Old Testament commandment that the Jews followed
>
> - and then provides a truth that both demonstrates their limited or incomplete view of God's holiness and reveals that truly God's standard is so much higher and holier than what they had ever thought or imagined.
>
> In verses 31-32, Jesus
>
> - first states an Old Testament commandment (setting aside the Jew's limited view of divorce)
>
> - and then provides a truth that both demonstrates their limited view of God's holiness and reveals God's standard—a standard that is so much higher and holier than they had ever thought or imagined.

Given this new understanding, we also see that the six "but I say to you statements" fit the context of the bookend statements of the passage—they are illustrations of how the righteousness of Jesus' followers must exceed that of the Pharisees and what the standard of being perfect means.

With each "but I say to you" statement, Jesus demonstrated that on our own, we cannot comprehend, much less satisfy, God's standard of holiness. This is the purpose of Jesus' words. This is the purpose of the sermon—to demonstrate that it is *impossible* for us to comprehend, to attain, or to satisfy God's standard of holiness!

With each example, Jesus demonstrates his listeners' error in thinking. Jesus is telling them, "You've been thinking God's standard of holiness is attainable at some human level. You think it is 'this high'—but God's standard for holiness is way beyond that; it is so much higher, so far beyond your comprehension that you cannot grasp it, and on your own, you can never meet it."

If the Jewish people thought that keeping the "You have heard" statements (do not murder, do not commit adultery, give a certificate of divorce, do not swear falsely, eye for an eye, tooth for a tooth, and love your neighbor) achieved God's perfect, holy standard, they were sorely mistaken, as Jesus' "but I say to you" statements made clear.

Each of Jesus' examples demonstrates the truth that God's holy standard is on such a high plane that it is beyond our human, earthly understanding, beyond our experience, beyond our capability.

There is a measure of comfort in Jesus' words when we recognize his teaching fits our human condition in such a true and matter-of-fact way. Even so, we know this does not mean we are getting away with anything; it does not mean our coming short of God's holiness is no big deal. Instead, we recognize that even if we very much want to please God, our reality and God's holy standard are far apart; the gap is vast and can never be bridged by human effort.

How then can our reality be reconciled to God's standard?

Resolution

As the people heard Jesus teach all these things, their reaction should have been, as ours should be, "God's holy standard is so much higher than I had ever thought or imagined. I cannot even begin to comprehend it. I cannot begin to meet it. I cannot satisfy it. How can I ever please God? How can I ever be perfect as the heavenly Father is perfect?"

Some of those listening to Jesus would have gone further in their thoughts, "Jesus is trying to tell me something. I'm not sure what it is except on the one hand, I have to be perfect and not break the least command and my righteousness must exceed that of the scribes and Pharisees, but on the other hand, Jesus has shown me it is impossible to do this. Maybe if I keep following him and listening to him, he'll tell me what it all means and what I need to do."

Consider that from the time of Moses, it was the norm the divorced would remarry; it had been the norm for 1,500 years. With this background, certainly some God-fearers who were listening to Jesus would have asked, "Why did God allow all this adultery to go on for 1,500 years? Why didn't Moses tell us this? We would not have remarried if we had known!"

These God-fearing Jews did not react this way because they knew Jesus was not making a rule, but instead, was teaching them something important. It is probable that at that time they did not know for sure what his point was, but they rightly sensed his teaching was not meant to be applied in a literal way.

What might Jesus say to reassure the crowd then—and reassure us now? The simple and wonderful reassurance is found in Jesus' own words in Matthew 5:17, "Do not think that I have come to abolish the Law or the Prophets; I have not come to abolish them but to fulfill them."

What Jesus meant when he said he came to fulfill the law is that he came to fulfill *every* "but I say to you" statement he made, and *every other* "but I say to you" statement he could have made. He came to fulfill the law to the farthest, highest, widest-reaching extent that is necessary to satisfy God's holiness.

"I have come...to fulfill them." These words are our great hope! Jesus fulfills the law, and he fulfills it for us.

Read these encouraging words of Paul as he describes how, by faith, we can have Jesus' righteousness credited to us,

Against all hope, Abraham in hope believed and so became the father of many nations, just as it had been said to him, "So shall your offspring be." Without weakening in his faith, he faced the fact that his body was as good as dead—since he was about a hundred years old—and that Sarah's womb was also dead. Yet he did not waver through unbelief regarding the promise of God, but was strengthened in his faith and gave glory to God, being fully persuaded that God had power to do what he had promised. This is why "it was credited to him as righteousness."

The words "it was credited to him" were written not for him alone, but also for us, to whom God will credit righteousness—for us who believe in him who raised Jesus our Lord from the dead. He was delivered over to death for our sins and was raised to life for our justification.   (Romans 4:18-25) NIV

and,

To the one who does not work, but believes on the One who justifies the ungodly, his faith is reckoned as righteousness.
(Romans 4:5) NIV

God will credit righteousness to us! This is the way a human being can be perfect—the only way—by God declaring that person righteous. God will credit righteousness to us who believe in Him who raised Jesus our Lord from the dead. This is the way our reality and God's holy standard are reconciled. What a wonder! And what a hope!

We read in Scripture, "The Law is a tutor to lead us to Christ" (Galatians 3:24). Matthew 5:17-48 is the most perfect fulfillment of Galatians 3:24—Christ himself, sitting on the mount, providing one example from the law after another, using the law as a tutor, using the law to show us we need something greater, using the law to bring us to himself, to Jesus Christ, to the very one who was speaking!

Matthew 5:17-48 is one of the most beautiful salvation passages in the Bible.

A Spiritual Application

As we walk on this earth, we fall short of the holiness God requires of us, in the things we should do and the things we should not do, in the things we should think and those we should not, in the things of which we are aware and the things of which we are unaware.

Many people believe that to be allowed into Heaven, their good works must outweigh their bad works, and they live accordingly, striving to have more good works in their account than bad. But when we grasp the salvation message in Matthew 5:17-48, we recognize that this is absolutely the wrong comparison to make!

The comparison is not between **our** good works and **our** bad works!

The correct comparison is between *our* **works** and *God's* **holy standard**!

Each of Jesus' "You have heard, but I say to you" illustrations compare our works to God's standard—his standard is that we must be perfect as our heavenly Father is perfect. We fall woefully short. There is no possible way *our* works can meet *God's* standard of holiness!

No matter how "good" we are, no matter how hard we try, on our own, it is impossible even to comprehend—much less attain or satisfy—God's holiness. Paul says, "If righteousness could be gained through the law, Christ died for nothing!" (Galatians 2:21b NIV). But because of our great God and Savior Jesus Christ, the totality of our sin and our coming short throughout our entire life is completely and absolutely covered with Jesus' righteousness.

Perhaps now, for the first time, you understand why you need Jesus' righteousness. Perhaps now, for the first time, you recognize that no matter how good you might be or how hard you try to do what is right, God's holy standard is beyond a human's ability to satisfy and each one of us completely misses it. Perhaps you are wondering how to have Jesus' righteousness given to you.

It is simple. Just accept it! Admit that your own efforts to be righteous fall feebly short of God's standard. Admit that you are a sinner against God. Then believe that his offer applies to you by trusting Jesus that he will credit his righteousness to you.

This is the simple gospel message. If you believe him and acknowledge that you fall short, if you believe he bore the burden by dying for your sins and that he rose from the dead, Jesus will cleanse you from all your unrighteousness. It would be good to talk to him about it right now. He already knows how far short you fall—admit it to him yourself. Then accept that Jesus covers your shortfalls and your sin with his righteousness.

After you believe, live by the transforming power of the Word of God and the leading of the Holy Spirit.

Practical Applications

Most of our Bibles have the word "except" in verse 32, and for most of us, that word might continue to cause us to read verses 31-32 incorrectly. It would be a good idea if we took a pencil, crossed out the word "except" and wrote in "besides." It would also be a good idea to put parentheses around the phrase as a reminder to de-emphasize it. These practical applications will help us read verses 31-32 correctly and will remind us every time we read this passage what is the point of Jesus' wonderful sermon—that we are incapable of comprehending or satisfying God's standard for holiness, and we need Jesus to credit us with his righteousness.

In addition, it might be helpful to make a note in the margin that reminds us this is a salvation message, not a list of rules for behavior. When we read through the examples in Matthew 5:17-48, we should not be mentally checking off, "I did this one. I missed this one. I'm good on this one." Instead, we should say, "I need Jesus' righteousness credited to me every day and in every circumstance."

PART II

Pharisees Confront Jesus – The Other Times Jesus Mentions Divorce

Matthew 19:3-12/Mark 10:2-12
Luke 16:14-18

5 | Jesus' Other Divorce Statements — an Introduction

Jesus spoke about divorce more than once in the gospels, but possibly not as often as we might think. Scripture records Jesus' words about divorce a total of four times:

- At the Sermon on the Mount (Matthew 5:31-32)
- To the Pharisees (Matthew 19:3-9/Mark 10:2-9)
- To the disciples (Matthew 19:10-12/Mark 10:10-12)
- A short statement reiterating earlier teaching (Luke 16:18)

There are three points to mention about these four occurrences. First, the Matthew 19 and Mark 10 verses are cross references and must be studied as one event; we will first discuss what Jesus said to the Pharisees and then we will discuss what Jesus said to his disciples.

Second, Jesus may have made the Luke 16:18 statement to the Pharisees or he may have been addressing all who were standing there; the context is not clear.

Third, the contexts of the first three occurrences are clear and each has a different context than the others. It is fundamental to our understanding that we be aware of the differences and take the context of each passage into account.

The following table (repeated from Chapter 1) reviews context differences in the first three occurrences.

Differences in the Contexts of Verses
Where Jesus Mentions Divorce

To the Crowds During the Sermon on the Mount Matthew 5:31-32	To the Pharisees When They Confronted Jesus Matthew 19:3-9/Mark 10:2-9	To The Disciples Later in a House Matthew 19:10-12/Mark 10:10-12
The verses are part of the Sermon on the Mount	The verses are not part of the Sermon on the Mount (nor in any of Jesus' discourses)	These verses record what Jesus said to the disciples privately in a house after the confrontation with the Pharisees
Jesus initiated the sermon	The Pharisees initiated the confrontation	The disciples asked a question that arose from the confrontation
Jesus sat down to speak and was intentional about a specific message	Jesus was responding to the Pharisees purposeful attempt to trap him	Jesus responded to the disciples' question about application
Jesus' audience was a receptive crowd	Jesus' audience was the antagonistic Pharisees	Jesus' audience was the disciples
The crowd recognized Jesus' authority, and realized it was an authority unlike their other teachers	The Pharisees were trying to undermine Jesus' authority	The disciples recognized Jesus' authority and were ready to learn and apply his teaching

In Matthew 19/Mark 10, Jesus mentions divorce during a confrontation with the Pharisees and then again later during a question and answer session with the disciples. The difference in Jesus' audience is significant because Jesus dealt very differently with the Pharisees than he did with followers—his disciples and the crowd at the Sermon on the Mount were receptive, the Pharisees were antagonistic; the others wanted to learn, the Pharisees wanted to trap him.[22]   When we take into account to whom Jesus was speaking and the context, we will have a more accurate understanding of why Jesus said what he did about divorce.

We will examine the Matthew 19/Mark 10 cross references in the rest of this chapter, but first, it is a good idea to read the passages (found in Appendix F).

An Exception Clause in Matthew 19:9?

Before considering these passages verse-by-verse, we will take a moment to discuss whether "except" is an accurate translation in Matthew 19:9 and whether there is an Exception Clause in the verse. A typical translation reads,

And I say to you, whoever divorces his wife, **except** *for sexual immorality, and marries another, commits adultery; and whoever marries her who is divorced commits adultery.*   (NKJV)

There is some uncertainty about the original Greek in Matthew 19:9, but of the two options, neither means "except." One of the two options is the word *parektos*, the same word used in Matthew 5:31-32; the other option, which is considered the more likely option, is *mē epi*. *Mē epi* (literally, "not on") is not translated "except" in Scripture. Examples of *mē epi* are found in the following verses (the words in italics indicate the translation of *mē epi*):

- Acts 4:17 "But so that it spreads *no* further *among* the people...
- Acts 24:4 "Nevertheless, *not* to be tedious *to* you any further..."
- Colossians 3:2 "Set your minds on the things above, *not on* the things of the earth."
- Revelation 7:16 "...*nor* the sun will beat down *on* them..."

---

[22]See Appendix C for background information about the Pharisees.

We can see *mē epi* is not translated as "except" in these verses nor is the idea of "except" found in these verses.

Using *mē epi* (the more likely option), the correct reading of Matthew 19:9 is,

"Whoever divorces his wife (*not for* immorality) and marries another, commits adultery against her."

This use of *mē epi* in Matthew 19:9 is a confirmation of the previous conclusion in Part I that "except" is not a translation we should use. As in Matthew 5:32, this clause is best understood placed in parentheses—Jesus is stating and setting aside the Jews' position about divorce.

We do not have an Exception Clause in Matthew 19:9. As we saw in Part I, and again here, the idea of an Exception Clause is not found at all in the Bible and should be dismissed from our minds.

The Matthew 19/Mark 10 Account Has Two Distinct Sections

The Matthew and Mark passages have, for the most part, the same elements in a slightly different order, but when reading the Matthew 19:3-12 and the Mark 10:2-12 cross references, it is key to recognize the narration naturally divides into two sections. The first section narrates the confrontation with the Pharisees. The second section narrates a short discussion Jesus had with his disciples following the confrontation with the Pharisees.

Similarly, we will divide our study into these two sections. We cover the first section (the confrontation with the Pharisees) in Chapters 6 and 7. We cover the second section (Jesus' discussion with his disciples) in Chapter 9. Chapter 8 connects the two sections by briefly discussing the Matthew 19:9 and Mark 10:11-12 cross-reference verses. These verses both mention divorce/remarriage/adultery and serve as a transition between Jesus' confrontation with the Pharisees and the discussion with his disciples.

Before we begin our discussion of Jesus' confrontation with the Pharisees, we will set the scene and organize the two accounts.

Setting the Scene

The Pharisees also came to Him, testing Him...   (Matthew 19:3a)
The Pharisees came...testing Him...   (Mark 10:2)

Very early in Jesus' ministry, the crowds recognized that Jesus spoke with authority, and they recognized that this was a departure from the manner of their teachers. We read at the conclusion of the Sermon on the Mount, "When Jesus had finished saying these things, the crowds were amazed at his teaching because he taught as one who had authority and not as their teachers of the law" (Matthew 7:28-29). The religious powers who were considered to have authority—the elders, the teachers of the law, the scribes, and the Pharisees—were well aware that the crowds had recognized the difference, and they resented Jesus' very real threat to their dominance and authority. They quickly became jealous of Jesus and continually attempted to damage his reputation with the hoped-for result of turning the crowds against Jesus.

Early on, these leaders had concluded they would have to contend openly with Jesus and come out ahead if they hoped to maintain their standing and authority with the crowds. Their goal was to make Jesus acknowledge, if not submit to, their authority, and when that did not work, ultimately their goal was to destroy him (Mark 3:1-6).

Scripture is clear as to the Pharisees' motivation in this passage as well; they were testing Jesus. Their questions were meant to show Jesus had not mastered, as they had, the whys, whens, and wherefores concerning the detailed particulars of divorce. Their main goal was to prove to the crowds that Jesus was unschooled and did not have a grasp of all the issues concerning divorce that were addressed in centuries of rabbinic tradition. They were confident Jesus' failure to pass their test would draw the crowds away from Jesus and back to themselves. It is essential to recognize this attitude of the Pharisees, not only in this passage, but whenever Jesus and the Pharisees have a confrontation. The Pharisees were not interested in learning from Jesus' answers nor were they interested in becoming followers of Jesus. Because of this, Jesus does not answer them in the same way he answered questions from his followers, from those who were seeking truth.

Organizing the Two Accounts

Matthew and Mark both recount this incident when the Pharisees confront Jesus, and they both tell us it was for the purpose of testing him. Although the two accounts have some variation, both writers include questions from the Pharisees and Jesus' comments (followed by Jesus' short discussion with his disciples).

Before going further, it will be helpful to harmonize the two accounts to make it clearer who said what and when because Matthew and Mark each arrange the passage slightly differently. In combining the accounts, we will follow Mark's order of events and identify six stages in the sequence of the confrontation between Jesus and the Pharisees.

Although it is possible to arrange the passage somewhat differently, going through it in the order below covers the main points in the clearest way. After that, we will consider the passage.

Stage 1

The Pharisees came and asked Him, "Is it lawful for a man to divorce his wife?" testing Him.   (Mark 10:2)

Is it lawful for a man to divorce his wife for just any reason?
(Matthew 19:3b)

Stage 2

Jesus answered them, "What did Moses command you?"
(Mark 10:3)

Stage 3

They said, "Moses permitted a man to write a certificate of divorce, and to dismiss her."   (Mark 10:4)

They said to Him, "Why then did Moses command to give a certificate of divorce, and to put her away?"   (Matthew 19:7)

Stage 4

Jesus said to them, "Because of your hardness of heart he wrote you this commandment."   (Mark 10:5)

He said to them, "Moses, because of the hardness of your hearts, permitted you to divorce your wives, but from the beginning it was not so."   (Matthew 19:8)

Stage 5

But from the beginning of the creation, God "made them male and female. For this reason a man shall leave his father and mother and be joined to his wife, and the two shall become one flesh" so then they are no longer two, but one flesh. Therefore what God has joined together, let not man separate."   (Mark 10:6-9)

And He answered and said to them, "Have you not read that He who made them at the beginning 'made them male and female,' and said, 'For this reason a man shall leave his father and mother and be joined to his wife, and the two shall become one flesh'? So then, they are no longer two but one flesh. Therefore what God has joined together, let not man separate."   (Matthew 19:4-6)

Stage 6

I say to you, whoever divorces his wife (not for sexual immorality) and marries another woman commits adultery, and whoever marries a divorced woman commits adultery. [23]   (Matthew 19:9)

We will consider these stages in the next chapter.

---

[23] Mark 10:10 will be discussed in Chapter 7, "Jesus' Explanation to His Disciples." Here in Matthew 19:9, we translate *mē epi* "not for."

6 | "What Did Moses Command You?"

We are ready now for a more detailed look at each stage of Jesus' confrontation with the Pharisees.

Divorce for Any Reason?

Stage 1

Is it lawful for a man to divorce his wife?   (Mark 10:2)

Is it lawful for a man to divorce his wife for just any reason?
(Matthew 19:3b)

At the time of Jesus, when it came to issues of divorce, there were two main schools of thought among the Pharisees. One group, the Hillels, held to easy divorce—a man could divorce his wife for almost any reason. The other group, the Shammais, held to a stricter code—a man could divorce his wife for very few reasons.[24] We do not know if these Pharisees were Shammais or Hillels or if they were a mix of the two, but it does not matter as far as this confrontation is concerned because they were not interested in furthering their knowledge and understanding. They were interested only in demonstrating to the crowds that Jesus did not understand all the arguments of each school of thought, and therefore, should not be considered a teacher worthy of respect and recognition.

The Pharisees' question "Is it lawful for a man to divorce his wife for just any reason?" (or "for any reason at all") was, in effect, "Do you hold to a long list of reasons like the Hillels? Or do you hold to a short list like the Shammais?"

---

[24] See Appendix B, *Divorce and Remarriage at the Time of Jesus,* for more information and background.

The Pharisees would have known all the arguments from both groups because they would have spent considerable time discussing and debating the topic, examining every argument in hairsplitting detail and coming up with many if-then scenarios concerning divorce.

Because of their so-called expertise, for whatever answer Jesus gave, the Pharisees thought they were well prepared to catch him in an opposing argument. Their purpose was to demonstrate to the crowds that Jesus did not have a grasp of the issues.

They were confident Jesus would not have good answers because this "knowledge" came only with years of tutelage under the rabbis and after much discussion and debate. They knew Jesus had not been discipled under any of the "expert" rabbis or Pharisees, and therefore, they were confident in their trap.[25]

Such a demonstration would prove Jesus had not mastered the rabbinical teachings as they had, and therefore, having failed the test, he was not worthy of having crowds of followers.

So then, what will Jesus answer? It appears he is in a "no-win situation." How will he answer the Pharisees' devious question?

Although most of us have never realized this—but of course, Jesus did—there was a basic problem with the Pharisees' question. Their question was faulty because it made an unwarranted assumption.

Their faulty logic gives Jesus the opportunity to take charge of the conversation, which, of course, he does.

---

[25] John 7:15 tells us, "And the Jews marveled, saying, 'How does this Man know letters, *having never studied?*'"

"What Did Moses Command You?"

Stage 2

Jesus answered them, "What did Moses command you?"

(Mark 10:3)

We should be delighted by this response from Jesus. It is the perfect question to challenge the Pharisees. "What did Moses command you?" is one of the most clever and astute statements in the Bible.

When Jesus counters the Pharisees, he is saying, "You consider yourselves experts in Moses' law and you call yourselves disciples of Moses; so then, you tell me what Moses commanded about this list."

Of course, if the Pharisees were truly experts in the law and disciples of Moses as they claimed (John 9:28), they would have no problem answering Jesus' question. Surely Moses' disciples would be able to state what Moses had commanded about the circumstances that allow divorce! Jesus' question, however, reveals something about divorce the Pharisees had not seemed to have realized, or possibly had not paid close enough attention, and "What did Moses command you?" gets to the heart of the issue.

What had the Pharisees not seemed to realize? They had not realized the fact that Moses *never* gave the Jewish people a list of reasons when a man could divorce his wife; *Moses had given no list*, short or long. The Pharisees, who proudly claimed to follow Moses so carefully, had made a completely faulty assumption—they wrongly assumed that Moses had a list and that their own list of reasons, whether the list was short or long, was in agreement with Moses.

Jesus *intended* his question to reveal the Pharisees' faulty assumption. They had no answer—because there was no list for them to recite.

The Pharisees were stopped in their tracks and taken aback. They had intended to undermine Jesus' authority, but instead of catching Jesus in a trap, he had confounded them and undermined *their* authority—and in front of the crowds!

Not easily deterred, and having much at stake, the Pharisees attempted to catch Jesus with another question, but again, the Pharisees were not asking for the purpose of ascertaining truth so they could apply Jesus' teaching to their lives. No, they reset the trap and tried again.

Moses and Divorce

Stage 3

They said, "Moses permitted a man to write a certificate of divorce, and to dismiss her."   (Mark 10:4)

They said to Him, "Why then did Moses command to give a certificate of divorce, and to put her away?"   (Matthew 19:7)

"Permit" and "Command"

Before we discuss the Pharisees' statements above, consider the use of the words "permit" or "allow" versus the word "command." It is important to recognize the distinction. Jesus, of course, is accurate in his use of the words, but the Pharisees seem to be unaware there is a distinction and confuse the words. The fact is, Moses *permitted* divorce and Moses *commanded* a certificate be given. We can see this in Jesus' use of the words. In Matthew 19:8, Jesus uses "permit" when he refers to divorce, "Moses...*permitted* you to divorce your wives," and in Mark 10:3-5, Jesus uses "command" when he refers to the certificate:

Verse 3—Jesus asks, "What did Moses *command* you?"

Verse 4—The Pharisees said, "Moses *permitted* a man to write a certificate of divorce, and to dismiss her."

Verse 5—Jesus says, "Because of your hard hearts, he wrote you this *commandment*."

In Mark 10:3-5, not only is Jesus accurate in his usage, he *corrects* the Pharisees.

Similarly to the Pharisees, the church also confuses the two, and in fact, we reverse the importance of them—we have made what *was allowed* (divorce) into commands and rules, and we have made what *was commanded* (a certificate) an afterthought, thereby missing the importance of the command. Divorce *was allowed*; the *command* was to give a certificate (Deuteronomy 24:1-4).

Jesus' incisive question, "What did Moses command you?" was designed to demonstrate that Moses never gave commands stating when a man could or should divorce his wife, and the Pharisees' inability to answer confirmed this.[26]

The Pharisees Try Again

Although the Pharisees were stumped by Jesus' question, they regrouped and again attempted to trap Jesus. The Pharisees' response in Stage 3 can be understood this way: "Moses allowed a man to write a certificate of divorce and send her away, but *why* did he say that?

The Pharisees' emphasis is on the "why"—"*Why* did Moses say to give her a certificate of divorce?" They want to know what Moses' reasons were. Here the Pharisees continue their logical fallacy—they wrongly reason that since Moses commanded to give a certificate of divorce, then Moses surely must also have had a list of reasons for when that divorce was allowed. However, just because Moses commanded that a certificate be given whenever a divorce occurred, it does not follow that Moses also had a list of reasons that enumerate when divorce is allowed.[27]

---

[26] In addition to the fact that Moses never gave commands stating when a man could or should divorce his wife, Scripture lists *only two* circumstances when divorce is forbidden, and these specifically apply *to men*—Deuteronomy 22:13-19 and Deuteronomy 22:28-29. See Appendix B for more information.

[27] Likewise, just because any one of us might agree a certificate of divorce should be given, it does not follow that we also have a list of reasons when divorce is allowed.

The Pharisees thought if they could successfully pressure Jesus to detail a list of why divorce is permitted, they could continue with their trap to show the crowds Jesus was not a competent teacher. However, Jesus did not fall into their trap.

Hard Hearts

Stage 4

Jesus said to them, "Because of your hardness of heart he wrote you this commandment." (Mark 10:5)

He said to them, "Moses, because of the hardness of your hearts, permitted you to divorce your wives, but from the beginning it was not so." (Matthew 19:8)

In Mark 10:5, Jesus used the word *commandment*, so we know he is talking about the certificate of divorce, and in Matthew 19:8, Jesus used the word *permitted* (or "allow"), and we know he is talking about the act of divorce. Jesus includes both divorce and the certificate in his "hard hearts" answer.

These words about hard hearts are in answer to what the Pharisees asked. "Moses allowed a man to write a certificate of divorce and send her away, but *why*? *What* were Moses' reasons?"

Jesus' answer is, in effect, "Here is the true situation: Moses wrote this because of your hard hearts."

Does Jesus' response seem harsh? It is harsh, but it is even harsher than we might think because Jesus phrased his response so his words were *not* a general statement. Instead, Jesus personalized it when he says, "*your* hardness...*you*...*your* wives." Remember that when Greek uses second person, it means "you," the person(s), or class of persons, being addressed. It does not mean third person, all people generally, as it is sometimes used in English. Here, Jesus is speaking directly to the Pharisees, which could also include others who were hard hearted in the same manner as the Pharisees, not just the individual Pharisees standing there.[28]

Jesus' answer using the second person helps us recognize Jesus was fully aware of what was going on—he knew the Pharisees' purpose was to trip him up in front of the crowds. He used the second person intentionally to direct his answer to them. The Pharisees wanted a list of rules; instead, Jesus reveals the condition of their hearts.

Let us consider how hard hearts tie into divorce, and especially how hard hearts tie into the certificate of divorce.

In some cultures at the time of Moses (and even today), a man could divorce his wife simply by saying, "I divorce you," and that would end the marriage. The lack of a certificate could present a problem for the wife. What if she wished to marry again, but no one believed her when she said that she was divorced? What if she wanted to enter a business contract or property transaction, but no one believed her when she said she was divorced and could act on her own? What if one day her ex-husband decided he still wanted to be married after all and showed up unexpectedly claiming he had never divorced her and she was still his wife (perhaps she had become wealthy or she was living a stable life and he wanted her to support him)?

There are many people who mean what they say—their word is their bond—but there are other people whose word is not to be trusted. Throughout history, many laws have been put into place to guard us from these untrustworthy people. Even if most of us are truthful, there are people who will lie and distort the truth. It is because of those people that, in court, the rest of us are required to swear "to tell the truth, the whole truth, and nothing but the truth." Many laws and rules are imposed on all of us simply because some are willing to lie, cheat, and defraud.

---

[28] In order to guard against making out-of-context applications, when Jesus uses the second person to a specific group, we should note who is addressed and not generalize the point.

In the same way, there are hard-hearted men who will say on one day, "I divorce you," but on another day will change their minds and attempt to go back on their word. Their word cannot be trusted. They have hard hearts. It is because of these people that a certificate of divorce was necessary and was commanded. This legal document certified the divorce and protected the woman.

When Jesus speaks to the Pharisees in the second person saying Moses commanded a certificate of divorce be given because of "*your* hard hearts," he is saying they are the very type of untrustworthy people who, when they divorce, make a divorce certificate necessary.[29]

This was another strong check on the Pharisees. Jesus again did not respond with one of the answers they anticipated. Instead of answering with a list of reasons when divorce is allowed, Jesus rebukes them by saying Moses commanded a certificate of divorce must be given because of "*your* hard hearts, because of people like *you.*"

For the Pharisees, this is another frustrating moment. Jesus humiliated them and completely differentiated their teachings, actions, and attitudes from those of Moses. They did not foresee this, and they were unprepared for Jesus' words. They were left dumbfounded and unable to argue with Jesus.

More About the Divorce Certificate

Did you know that at the time of Moses, the Jewish divorce certificate was unique? In just a few other cultures at that time, only a few privileged women were allowed to have a certificate of divorce.[30] Although the Israelites' marriage customs were similar to the nations around them, the Jews were the only culture where it was

---

[29] Some think Jesus' hard hearts statement means that if a couple is divorced, it proves that the husband and/or wife had a hard heart, but this is not supportable from these verses. Jesus says the Pharisees (and those like the Pharisees) have hard hearts; he does not say hard hearts cause divorce.

[30] David Instone-Brewer, *Divorce and Remarriage in the Bible* (Grand Rapids: William B. Eerdmans Publishing Company, 2002), 32-33

commanded that all women in divorce situations must receive a certificate of divorce.[31]

The Jewish divorce certificate verified a woman was divorced, which proved the ex-husband had no claim on her. Besides certifying she was a free woman who would then be able to transact business and act on her own, the certificate specifically stated that she was free to marry again. Truly, the God-given, Jewish divorce certificate was a revolutionary document, a document that was specifically designed for the protection and welfare of women. Further, this provision allows everyone to witness God's high view of women and his concern for them.

Although we may tend to think of the divorce certificate in a negative light, we should not. Jewish women over many centuries have found it a blessing that safeguarded their rights and protected them from being taken advantage of by manipulative or dishonest (hard-hearted) ex-husbands. In fact, throughout the centuries, the divorce certificate has brought freedom and security to thousands upon thousands of women, even outside of Judaism, that they would never have had without it. All women in every culture who have been protected in this way owe a debt of gratitude to Moses and to our great God who is concerned about all women.

---

[31] Again, it might not seem clear to us when we read Deuteronomy 24:1-4 in our English Bibles that it was a command to give a certificate of divorce, but Jesus makes it clear—the Greek used in Matthew 5:31 for "give" is a command. Further, one reason we may have misunderstood Jesus' purpose in the Matthew 5:17-48 discourse is because we did not realize the certificate of divorce was *commanded*. Matthew 5:31 is one of the six commands Jesus used to make his point.

7 "Let Not Man Separate" or Who Can Divorce? How Is It Decided?

"From the Beginning" and "Let Not Man Separate"

Stage 5

But from the beginning of the creation, God 'made them male and female. For this reason a man shall leave his father and mother and be joined to his wife, and the two shall become one flesh' so then they are no longer two, but one flesh. Therefore what God has joined together, let not man separate."   (Mark 10:6-9)

Have you not read that He who made them at the beginning "made them male and female," and said, "For this reason a man shall leave his father and mother and be joined to his wife, and the two shall become one flesh"? So then, they are no longer two but one flesh. Therefore what God has joined together, let not man separate.
(Matthew 19:4-6)

Next, Jesus uses the Old Testament to describe marriage. None of the Jews listening to Jesus, including the Pharisees, would disagree with these words. God created males and females, and God established the marriage relationship (Genesis 1:27, 5:2, 2:24).

What caused a problem for the Pharisees were the words in Jesus' reply that are *not* found in the Old Testament, "What God has joined together, let not man separate" (or "let no man separate").

If asked, "What do the words, 'What God has joined together, let not man separate' mean?" many Christians will answer (perhaps somewhat uncertainly), "It means we should not divorce." But this would be an effortless and superficial assumption for us to make, and it has three difficulties.

One, most Christians agree the Bible does allow divorce. We might differ when it is allowed, but most of us agree Scripture does indicate divorce is allowed. Therefore, it would be inconsistent to assume Jesus' statement, "What God has joined together, let no man separate" means we should not divorce.

Two, the command, "What God has joined together, let no man separate," is found only in this confrontation; *it is found nowhere else in Scripture*. Further, Jesus was not teaching this to his followers or to a receptive crowd like the one listening to the Sermon on the Mount in Matthew 5. Jesus said this as a retort to Pharisees who were confronting him.

Three, there is another meaning of this command that better fits the context. We take a step toward understanding what Jesus meant when we keep in mind that the Pharisees thought of themselves as the arbiters of most Jewish life issues—that they considered themselves to be the ones with insight and understanding, and they considered their rulings should be deemed authoritative for the masses in issues of daily life and religion, which, of course, included divorce. Once we realize the Pharisees claimed the religious authority to say under what circumstances a husband and a wife could divorce, then we begin to understand how this command would challenge their position.

Indeed, Jesus challenged the Pharisees' self-appointed authority with this command. Jesus used the word *anthropos*, meaning "man" or "human being" (male or female). "What God has joined together, let no human being separate."

Jesus is contrasting mere man with the Almighty God. God created marriage and God is the one who joins a couple together in marriage. The idea is, "If God joins a couple, and everyone agrees this is the case, then who is a human being to say when a couple can divorce? How did the Pharisees, mere *men*, obtain such an authority that they can separate something *God* has joined together?"

Picture Jesus developing his argument—

"Have you not read that He who created them from the beginning made them male and female," and everyone nods their heads at these familiar words.

"For this reason a man shall leave his father and mother and be joined to his wife." Again, everyone agrees with this Old Testament statement describing marriage; a new family unit begins.

"And the two shall become one flesh. So they are no longer two, but one flesh." And again, all nod their heads understanding that in marriage and in the sexual relationship, two individuals become one.

No one would disagree with anything Jesus said; in fact, they are all in agreement. They revere the words of the Old Testament.

Then Jesus quashes the Pharisees, *"No human* has authority to separate a marriage *God* created."

Reactions to this statement likely included silence, anger, or awe.

The Pharisees had usurped an authority that belongs to God alone. The correct way to think is, "What God has joined, God alone separates." No Pharisee, or any other human authority, has the right to separate what God has joined together.

Jesus' command includes the word "therefore." "Therefore, what God has joined together, let no man separate." The "therefore" lets us know this is the summation and answer to the Pharisees' original question. The Pharisees' original question was, "Is it lawful for a man to divorce his wife for any reason?" Jesus' answer, "What *God* has joined together, let no *human* separate," means "It's not up to you—mere human beings—to decide who can separate." Jesus used the "let no man separate" command to challenge the Pharisees' self-appointed authority that they are the ones who determine if a couple can divorce. Pharisees should not decide when a divorce is allowed, and they should not decide for a couple if they can divorce.

Jesus' "therefore" statement renders irrelevant both the Pharisees' request for a list of reasons and their question whether it is lawful for a man to divorce his wife for any reason.

Two Points of Grammar

We should consider two points of grammar about Jesus' words "Let no man separate." First, it is clear in the Greek that this is an imperative, (i.e., a command); we might not fully realize it is a command because of the use of the word "Let." Make no mistake, Jesus gave a command.

Second, notice Jesus' use of third person here. He included other people besides these Pharisees. He uses the third person because he is making a command that goes beyond the Pharisees. He commanded, "Let no human separate a marriage."

Although Jesus' answer strips the power from the Pharisees (who were the ones ruling on divorce issues at that time), the use of third person strips the authority from any who would claim such authority today—from all who would decide for a couple if they are allowed to divorce. When Jesus stated this command, it was initially directed to the Pharisees, but his use of the third person lets us know it is also directed to anyone who might be tempted to take on such authority. There is *no place* in the Bible that gives one person the authority to say when or if another person can divorce. In fact, we see in Jesus' words to the Pharisees it is just the opposite. Only God has this authority, and it is up to each person to seek the Lord's will in his or her situation. This is the purpose of the "Let no human separate" command. It is not a statement explaining if or when divorce is allowed.

Notice that this command does not prohibit divorce. It states that no human being has the authority to say when or if a man or woman can divorce.

Jesus' Confrontation with the Pharisees— Summary Points

Let us summarize what we have learned about divorce from Jesus' confrontation with the Pharisees.

First, by Jesus' incisive question, "What did Moses command you?" Jesus exposed the Pharisees' faulty logic, and we discovered Moses did not give a list of reasons when a couple can divorce.

Second, we learned that Mosaic Law *allowed* divorce and it *commanded* that when a divorce occurred, a certificate must be given (which provided unheard of protections for women).

Third, Jesus said the certificate of divorce was commanded because of the hard hearts of Pharisees and people like them.

Fourth, "Let no man separate," is a command in the third person; it applies to all of us. It tells us that no mere human, no layperson or church leader, has the authority to say if a man or woman can divorce.

Fifth, notice that Jesus does not prohibit divorce—he simply says no human has the authority to say if a couple is allowed to divorce.

Lastly, notice that Jesus did not state a list of his own. Thus we see that in Matthew 5, and now in Mark 10/Matthew 19, Jesus gave no list stating when divorce and/or remarriage is allowed.

Who Can Divorce? How Is It Decided?

Scripture does allow divorce, but we are left with the questions, "Who is allowed to divorce?" "How is it decided?"

At the time Jesus arrived on the scene, it was the Pharisees who answered these questions and made pronouncements concerning divorce for the people. But with the "let no man separate" command, Jesus took the authority out of the Pharisees' hands and out of human hands.

Rather than asking for a list of reasons *why* someone can divorce, we see from Jesus' "Let no man separate" command that the Pharisees would have asked a better question if they had asked Jesus, "*Who* decides if a couple can divorce?"

Asking "Who decides?" helps redirect us to the bigger question, "Who decides any of the various issues that arise in a believer's life?" The answer is God alone knows the answers to any and all questions about behavior, and in the new covenant, God uses the transforming power of his Word and the leading of the Holy Spirit to direct and guide each individual Christian to the correct answers and choices in life. What a wonder this loving, caring attention and direction from our Lord is, and we are thankful for it.

We believers are recipients of the attention and direction God lovingly gives to each of us individually, and because we all differ from one another—coming to Christ at different stages and circumstances of life, having various backgrounds and cultures, having diverse strengths, weaknesses, intellects, and emotional makeup—it makes sense that God works with us individually and in various ways.

Likewise, each marriage and each couple is uniquely different from every other marriage and couple. Just as we have seen God lead, guide, and work with each of us individually and uniquely, we should expect God will also work with each marriage in a unique way. When a marriage is in trouble, we should expect God would also deal uniquely with that marriage. We should expect God might have one couple remain married and work through a certain issue but allow another couple to divorce for that same issue. *God alone* knows the hearts and the circumstances of the individuals involved.

Just as we discussed in Matthew 5, each individual is led by the Word and the Holy Spirit to decide the issues of his or her own behavior. So too, it is the man and woman in a troubled marriage, with the guidance of the Word and the Holy Spirit, who each have the solemn responsibility to hear what God says about whether or not God has separated his or her marriage. Just as in any other area of our lives, the more time we spend in the Word, the better we will hear God's guidance for the decisions we make.

The Pharisees' Reaction

The Pharisees had endeavored to entangle Jesus in an argument hoping to expose him as an untrained teacher, but their attempt to trap Jesus was a failure, as were all their tests.

In this confrontation, Jesus' statements expose the Pharisees as not understanding Moses or the issues of divorce, remove them from their self-appointed position of authority, and firmly establish Jesus' own authority. The Pharisees would have recognized immediately that Jesus' answers were perceptive and that he successfully redirected their questions. He revealed their hard-heartedness, and he had exposed to all that they had been acting without God-given authority. We might even say Jesus' answers were living and active, revealing the thoughts and attitudes of their hearts.

The Pharisees would have been devastated and humiliated, their authority completely destroyed—and in front of everybody. Not only did the Pharisees lose this battle about divorce, they lost the entire war—anyone paying attention would have seen it. This made them more furious and more determined than ever to stop Jesus. As we better understand how thoroughly Jesus destroyed their arguments and status, we get an even clearer insight into why they were so determined to stop Jesus and why they eventually planned to kill him.

8 | From Confrontation to Explanation

Whoever Divorces and Marries Another Commits Adultery

We are in the midst of considering the second and third of the four times Jesus said that remarriage after divorce is adultery (the four are listed on page 67). Now we have come to the verses in Matthew 19/Mark 10 that connect divorce to adultery. These verses also function as a transition between Jesus' confrontation with the Pharisees and his discussion with his disciples.

Jesus' statements from Matthew 19 and Mark 10:

I say to you, "Whoever divorces his wife (not for immorality) and marries another woman commits adultery, and whoever marries a divorced woman commits adultery."[32] (Matthew 19:9)

And in the house the disciples asked him again about this matter. And he said to them, "Whoever divorces his wife and marries another commits adultery against her. And if a woman divorces her husband and marries another, she commits adultery." (Mark 10:11-12)

In the Matthew 19 passage, "I say to *you*" was spoken to the Pharisees so "you" refers to the Pharisees (which we referred to as "Stage 6"). In the Mark 10 passage, the scene switches to later in a house when the disciples have a short discussion with Jesus, so "He said to *them*" was spoken to the disciples.

We might wonder why these accounts differ in this regard. One scenario that explains this difference is that when Jesus made his statement to the Pharisees, it was the last thing he said to them,

---

[32] Here in Matthew 19:9, we have translated *mē epi* "not for." See Chapter 5.

and then later with his disciples, Jesus reframed the last comment they heard him say to the Pharisees.

Jesus did not include the "not for immorality" clause in his statement to the disciples because the disciples had already understood the purpose of such a clause when Jesus used *parektos* at the Sermon on the Mount. Instead, what we see is that the disciples react strongly to Jesus' words about divorce, remarriage, and adultery, and the discussion in the house focused on that concern.

Review of the Second Context Mistake

At this point, we want to recall from Chapter 1 the discussion regarding the second context mistake—inappropriately combining Matthew 5:31-32 with other gospel verses just because these other verses mention divorce and adultery. But simply because two sets of verses use similar words, it does not mean they have the same implication and intent. Our example, "You should wear black," could have different meanings depending on the context. We can see that concept plainly illustrated with the divorce verses, and we are at the point where we can contrast Jesus' statements:

- from the Sermon on the Mount in Matthew 5:31-32

- during his confrontation with the Pharisees in Matthew 19:9

- to his disciples in Mark 10:11-12

Let us reread the statements themselves.

To the crowds at the Sermon on the Mount: Jesus said,
 It was said, "Anyone who divorces his wife must give her a certificate of divorce." But I say to you, anyone who divorces his wife (besides for immorality) causes her to commit adultery, and anyone who marries a divorced woman commits adultery.
(Matthew 5:31-32)

To the Pharisees during the confrontation: Jesus said,
 I tell you that anyone who divorces his wife (not for immorality) and marries another commits adultery."
(Matthew 19:9)

To the Disciples after the confrontation: Jesus said,

And he said to them, "Whoever divorces his wife and marries another commits adultery against her. And if a she divorces her husband and marries another, she commits adultery."

(Mark 10:11-12)

To the Crowds at the Sermon on the Mount

When Jesus made his divorce/remarriage/adultery statement to the receptive crowd at the Sermon on the Mount, he was not listing rules for his followers by which to live. His purpose was to use the statement as one of six examples to instruct the crowds that, on their own, they could never attain God's holy standard of righteousness. That crowd of followers did not take Jesus' words literally but understood he was telling them something of great importance (even if at that time, they might not have been quite sure what it all meant). Matthew 5:17-48 is a salvation message!

To the Pharisees

When Jesus made this statement to the Pharisees, he revealed significant difficulties in their position. The Pharisees had wrongly appropriated for themselves the authority to approve divorces. Jesus corrected them and stated that they had no such authority, and in fact, he made it clear that no human has such authority. Furthermore, in appropriating the authority to approve divorces, the Pharisees would have been responsible for the dissolution of many marriages that God would have wanted to keep together, and they had, by extension, approved the remarriages and thus would be responsible for the myriad of adulteries that resulted from the subsequent marriages.

The disciples, and anyone else listening in on this conversation, would have found Jesus' comments and his exchange with the Pharisees fascinating, if not startling. A few might possibly have found it humorous as the Pharisees were exposed as not understanding Moses!

Jesus' statement provided the Pharisees a perfect opportunity to ask Jesus what he meant and to ask how they might apply his words, but Pharisees will not do this. They were not interested in an explanation, and they did not ask any questions about this statement. Because they were so confident in their own righteousness and so intent on maintaining their position of religious power and authority, they refused to recognize they were sinners and lost and in desperate need of help and so did not ask the necessary questions or seek the help they needed.

To the Disciples

After Jesus' confrontation with the Pharisees ended, when he was with the disciples in the house, he began teaching and explaining. Jesus knew his disciples (and we) might not understand the last comment he had just made to the Pharisees, and in order to clear up confusion, he allowed them to ask their question so he could specifically address this issue. He did this to initiate a teaching time with his disciples, and he began by reframing his statement.

As Jesus anticipated, when the disciples heard these words, they reacted with alarm, but then appropriately, they asked Jesus about it. In the next chapter, we will consider Jesus' explanation to his disciples, those who truly wanted to know how best to follow Jesus.

9 | Jesus Answers His Disciples' Questions

The conversation up to this point had been between Jesus and the Pharisees, those opposing him. Jesus' disciples, however, had been listening receptively, and we now turn to the second phase of the narration that covers the short conversation Jesus had with his disciples.

Alone with His Disciples

In the house ... (Mark 10:10)

After the confrontation with the Pharisees ends, Jesus and his disciples move into a house. This is an important point and not to be overlooked. Jesus often had private times with his disciples and followers when he clarified or explained something he had just said. For example, we see a similar situation in Matthew 15:7-20 (and its cross reference in Mark 7:17) where Jesus moved into a house with the disciples and further explained his teaching about clean and unclean foods. We also see that after the short parable of the sower, Jesus took a good deal of time to answer questions and to explain to his followers and the twelve when they were separated from the crowd (Mark 4:10).

Not only did Jesus take time to answer the disciples' questions separately, but he told them he spoke in parables because the mysteries of the kingdom of Heaven had not been given to others (Matthew 13:10-15). In the same way, Jesus now has a conversation with his followers that leaves out the Pharisees. Paying attention to the phrase "in the house" prevents us from muddling together conversations Jesus has with antagonists and those he has with followers.

Also, remember in Chapter 2 of this book, we mentioned that it would have been helpful if someone had asked Jesus about his

Matthew 5:31-32 statement, and we pointed out that the disciples would later become confused and would ask Jesus about his divorce/remarriage/adultery words. We are now at that point.

Here, in the house, the disciples question Jesus about his statement, and to clear up their confusion, he explains whether the verses are meant to be applied literally. His answer is indispensable in the divorce/remarriage/adultery question.

Are you ready for Jesus' explanation?

"Whoever Divorces His Wife..."

...the disciples asked him again about this matter. And he said to them, "Whoever divorces his wife and marries another commits adultery against her. And if a woman divorces her husband and marries another, she commits adultery."   (Mark 10:11-12)

When Jesus made a similar statement to the Pharisees (in Matthew 19:9), it was the last thing he said to them, and it ended their conversation. Shortly after this, when he was in the house with his disciples, they questioned him about what he had said, and Jesus begins by reframing his statement.

The disciples asked because they wanted to understand. The chief difference between Jesus' followers' questions and the Pharisees' questions is that followers ask so they can understand and apply the answer to their own lives; Pharisees do not— understanding and application is not their goal.

For those who are teachable, such as the disciples and other followers, Jesus' statement allowed for discussion and learning. The disciples were seekers of truth and desired more information. They wondered about the ramifications of Jesus' words and reacted with alarm.

The Disciples' Radical Conclusion

"If such is the case of the man with his wife, it is better not to marry."   (Matthew 19:10)

This statement by the disciples is further evidence that they understood Jesus' words in Matthew 5:31-32 were not meant to be applied literally. When Jesus said his divorce words in the Sermon on the Mount, neither the disciples nor the crowd questioned Jesus. At that time, they understood Jesus was not giving rules for behavior. There was no evidence that the disciples or the crowds understood his words should be applied literally or that anyone voiced concerns or questions, nor is there any evidence of the social upheaval that would have occurred if the crowd understood they should literally apply Jesus' words as consequences for behavior.

If anyone had asked Jesus about this at the Sermon on the Mount, there would be no need to ask now because they would have already known the answer. However, in a different setting, it seems doubts arose when Jesus uttered these words. Perhaps when the disciples heard Jesus make a similar statement, they did a double take and thought, "Maybe Jesus really does mean a person would become a literal adulterer if he or she remarries after divorce, and therefore, shouldn't remarry." This is the only time they assumed that Jesus might expect that these words should be applied literally, and unlike the Pharisees, the disciples do the reasonable thing—they ask Jesus about it.

Before we consider Jesus' answer, there are two interesting points about this verse that are not usually brought out in a discussion of this passage.

Aitia

The first point is the word translated in verse 10 as "case." The Greek is *aitia*. *Aitia* is used twenty times in the Greek New Testament and two of those are in our Matthew 19:3-12 passage.

The definitions from the Greek lexicon are "reason," "cause," "charge," "ground for complaint," "accusation."[33] In the Greek New Testament, the uses of *aitia* fall into two groups. Not counting our text, nine translate simply as "reason," and nine have to do with a legal situation.

Examples of *aitia* translated "reason":

- Paul, to Jewish leaders in Rome: "For this *reason*, I called you to see and speak with you..." (Acts 28:20)

- Paul, to Timothy: "For this *reason*, I remind you to fan into flame the gift of God." (2 Timothy 1:6)

- Paul, to the men sent from Cornelius: "I'm the one you are seeking. What is the *reason* you are here?" (Acts 10:21)

Examples of *aitia* translated using legal terms:

- Pilate, to the Jews, "I find no ground for *an accusation* against him." (John 18:38b, 19:4, 6)

- "The *charge* against him was written in Hebrew, Latin, and Greek." (Matthew 27:37)

- Festus, to King Agrippa about Paul: "They did not bring an *accusation* that I was expecting." (Acts 25:18)

- Paul, to the Jewish leaders in Rome: "They examined me and wanted to release me because there was no *charge* worthy of death against me." (Acts 28:18)

---

[33] Walter Bauer, *A Greek-English Lexicon of the New Testament and Other Early Christian Literature, 3rd ed.* Revised and Edited by Frederick William Danker. (BDAG) (Chicago: The University of Chicago Press, 2000). BDAG's option of "relationship" is not demanded and is an unnecessary stretch for the meaning of *aitia.*

Of the two uses of *aitia* in Matthew 19:3-12, the first is in verse 3 and translates "reason." "Is it lawful for a man to divorce his wife for just any reason?"

The second use of *aitia* is in verse 10, and in this verse has the meaning used for legal situations. Remember, the seventh commandment says, "Thou shalt not commit adultery." Those Jews who committed adultery were considered guilty of breaking the seventh commandment. For the Jews, adultery was a legal accusation and a punishable offense carrying a death sentence in the Mosaic law.[34]

When the disciples, as Jews, hear Jesus' words in Mark 10:11-12, "*Whoever divorces his wife and marries another commits adultery against her. And if a woman divorces her husband and marries another, she commits adultery,*" they offer a tentative conclusion that seems reasonable, "If such is the accusation (*aitia*) against the man regarding his wife, it is better not to marry again." They make an assumption based on their cultural background that Jesus means the couple would be guilty of breaking the commandment and would be guilty of the *charge* of committing adultery. Thus, the disciples mean, "If it would be a (legal) charge of adultery against this husband regarding his wife, then wouldn't it be better not to remarry after divorce?"

When we consider this cultural understanding of *aitia*, we have a better grasp of the disciples' concern. It should cause us to realize the disciples thought it might be an issue of Jewish law.

"It is better..."

The second and more important point not to miss in Matthew 19:10 is the disciples' use of the word "better." The disciples say, "It is *better* not to marry." They mean that although remarriage after divorce had never been considered to be adultery—after all, the

---

[34] Instone-Brewer states that there is no record of the death penalty for adultery ever being applied in the first century C.E. and was probably never inflicted in the New Testament era. David Instone-Brewer, *Divorce and Remarriage in the Bible* (Grand Rapids: William B. Eerdmans Publishing Company, 2002), 94

Jews had been remarrying after divorce for centuries—they conclude, based on Jesus' statement, that if remarriage would actually be considered grounds for a case of adultery, it would be *better* not to remarry after divorce.

The first part of the disciples' statement displays their cultural understanding of the seriousness of an adultery charge; the second part displays what actions they believe should be taken to avoid the charge—it would be *better* not to marry again after divorce.

Although we Christians today are not under the law and thus do not have the same cultural understanding of adultery the Jewish disciples did, many of us think in a similar way as the disciples—although it might be permissible to marry after divorce, it would be *better* not to marry since it is adultery. Are we right to say that while it might be allowed, still it is *better* not to remarry after divorce?

Is it, in fact, better not to marry again after divorce? Were the disciples right? Are *we* right? Is it *better*?

Who Is the Divorce/Adultery Statement For?

Jesus answered the disciples,

All cannot accept this saying, but only those to whom it has been given: For there are eunuchs who were born thus from their mother's womb, and there are eunuchs who were made eunuchs by men, and there are eunuchs who have made themselves eunuchs for the kingdom of heaven's sake. He who is able to accept it, let him accept it.   (Matthew 19:11-12)

What is Jesus referring to when he says, "this saying?" Is it "Whoever divorces his wife and marries another commits adultery against her" or is it the disciples' response "It is better not to marry?" Because Jesus explains by describing eunuchs—who do not marry—"this saying" most likely refers to "It is better not to marry."

Graciously, Jesus corrects the disciples' misapplication of his teaching. He responds to their concern and tells them that while their conclusion "better not to marry" is mistaken in general, it is appropriate for a few. Jesus' eunuch teaching explains what the disciples (and we) need to know.

To us, Jesus' statement about eunuchs may seem cryptic; however, it was not cryptic to the disciples. Although just two verses long, it will take us a few pages to explain Jesus' straightforward meaning.

The word translated "accept" is the Greek word *chōreō* and has the meaning "make room for." We will use the translation "make room for" because it is accurate and because the translation "accept" tends to throw some of us off track by causing us to focus on the word "accept." "Accept" may have more of the idea "I must do this," while "make room for" has more of the idea of "If it is possible."

When we know the phrase is "make room for," the words make much more sense.

A closer translation of verses 11-12 says,

"Not all *can make room* for this statement but those to whom it has been given. For there are eunuchs who from the womb of their mother were born thus, and there are eunuchs who were made eunuchs by men, and there are eunuchs who made themselves eunuchs for the sake of the kingdom of heaven. The one who is able *to make room, let him make room.*"

The statement about eunuchs has three main phrases that help us zero in on those who are the ones who can make room for Jesus' statement in verses 11-12.

1) Those to whom it has been given make room for the statement "it is better not to marry."

There are only certain people who can make room for Jesus' statement—the ones to whom it has been given. This phrase tells us *not everyone is included.* It is not necessarily good or bad, and it does not teach us that anyone must change himself or herself; Jesus' statement is for some and not others. It is for "those to whom it has been given."

2) Eunuchs make room for the statement that "it is better not to marry."

The typical meaning of eunuch is a male who has been castrated, leaving him with very little or no sexual desire. Such a person could have been intentionally made a eunuch because he was to work in a harem or other position that required someone with no sexual desire. Then too, some males are physically born eunuchs from a birth defect. Not many males would be included in this group, but then, eunuchs are rare in general. Still others decide to "eunuch themselves" for the kingdom of heaven, which means they do not marry so they can more fully serve God. Although the first two examples do not include females, if we understand Jesus to be making a teaching point, then the third group could include women who decide not to marry for the kingdom of heaven.

However, no matter which of the three we mean, when eunuch is mentioned, we automatically think of sex, and very specifically, the lack of sexual desire. *The lack of sexual desire is the identifying characteristic of a eunuch.*

Now, back to the passage. The word "for" connects eunuchs with "those to whom it has been given,"

"...*to those to whom it has been given.* **For** *there are eunuchs who...*"

The eunuch phrase explains "to whom it has been given" and narrows the field further to a relatively small group of people—eunuchs. The "to whom" in Jesus' comment refers to eunuchs.

3) Those who are able make room for the statement "it is better not to marry."

We tend to let this phrase slip right past without recognizing its importance. The point is, only certain people have the ability to make room for not marrying; only certain people will *be able* to give up a sexual relationship. Others will not be able to make room for giving up a sexual relationship, which is fine.

These three points give us criteria of those who make room for not marrying, and there is no getting around the fact that the three points add up to a sexual situation. Because sexual attraction is so strong and so common to the human experience, the ones who make room for this statement that it is better not to marry are those who meet all three criteria, a relatively small group:

1) those to whom it has been given *and*
2) those who are "eunuchs" *and*
3) those who are able

Jesus did not put any pressure on anyone to make room for the eunuch statement. To be one of the people Jesus is talking about here (i.e., to be one of the people for whom this conclusion "it is better not to marry" applies), all three criteria must be met.

The Eunuch Statement and the Divorced

Now we will consider how Jesus' eunuch statement comes to bear for a divorced person. In order for the divorced person to make room for this *"it is better not to marry"* situation, he or she would:

1) have to be one of the people to whom the statement had been given

and

2) have to eunuch themselves, i.e., they decide for themselves not to marry (men and women)

and

3) be able not to be married—they are able to give up a sexual relationship.

Unless a divorced person decides to eunuch himself or herself for the kingdom of heaven, he or she is not a part of this group.[35]

---

[35] The phrase "to eunuch himself or herself" does not mean "a vow of chastity" is required, as in a promise to never marry again, i.e., a permanent situation. It does mean a person might realize he or she is okay *for now* without sex. Later, if the situation changes, he or she is free to marry.

However, when the church tells a divorced person he or she cannot remarry, *the church is trying to force that person into becoming a eunuch*—assuming an authority *never* assigned to the church. It would be going too far for anyone to tell a divorced person not to remarry because that would be equivalent of making that person a eunuch!

On the other hand, Jesus does say a divorced person can eunuch himself; he can decide for himself not to remarry. But—it is the divorced person himself or herself who decides if he or she has been given the ability to say no to sexual attraction and passion. It is not up to the church, and it is not up to a leader in the church. Only the divorced person himself or herself could possibly know if it has been given and if he or she is able to give up a sexual relationship.

The disciples understood this is what Jesus meant and did not ask another question because this answer satisfied. Why would this statement satisfy the disciples?

1) It explains that their radical conclusion was wrong, that rejecting or avoiding remarriage after divorce was *not better* for most divorced people, and that divorced people could marry again if, for example, sexual attraction was the reason they wanted to remarry.[36]

2) It states that only a few specific divorced people will decide not to marry again, or looking at it the other way, most divorced people will decide to remarry. Indeed, since eunuchs are rare, not many will choose to remain unmarried.

3) It says that divorced people will choose for themselves not to marry again, but this applies to those who are able to be a eunuch of sorts, a person with no sexual desire.

4) It reinforces their prior understanding that Jesus did not mean these words were to be applied literally.

---

[36] There can be other reasons why a divorced person might want to marry again besides sexual reasons (e.g., companionship or raising a family). Jesus addresses just one reason here, sexual passion.

Why Did Mark Not Include the *Mē Epi* Clause?

Some have wondered why the Mark 10 passage leaves out the phrase "not for immorality" that is found in Matthew 19:9. We have seen that in the three divorce passages we have examined, the traditional Jewish understanding/position about divorce for immorality is de-emphasized. In Matthew 5:32, *parektos* de-emphasizes the clause. In Matthew 19:9, *mē epi* de-emphasizes the clause. Mark de-emphasizes the clause simply by eliminating it altogether. For Mark, omitting it is a non-issue; omitting it was simply Mark's way to de-emphasize the clause.

Why Did Mark Not Include the Eunuch Statement?

Why did Mark not include the section about eunuchs? We cannot know for certain, of course, but one likely reason would be because Mark's focus was on the confrontation with the Pharisees rather than that the divorced can marry again. But why would the confrontation with the Pharisees be Mark's focus?

The Pharisee section would be the more critical point to narrate because this is where a profound change in a believer's relationship with God is demonstrated. We might not immediately see the importance of this if we do not grasp how intrusive and overbearing into almost every area of life was the Pharisees' control and authority. In this section, we see Jesus stripping the Pharisees' authority they had wrongly appropriated. He did this with his command, "What God has joined together, let no man separate." For the sake of his followers at that time, and for our sake now, Jesus stripped the power from the Pharisees and from anyone else who would wield such "religious" authority over us.[37]

This was a profound change in the way believers would relate to God, and of utmost importance to recount. Church leaders do not

---

[37] Matthew's Gospel also emphasizes the stripping of the Pharisees' authority; it does so by placing "What God has joined together, let no man separate" *first* in the arrangement of the topics covered.

have this authority over us.[38] This is wonderful news! When we become new creatures in Christ, we have a new authority—Jesus Christ himself is our authority, and he guides us by the transforming power of the Word of God and the leading of the Holy Spirit.

In addition, Mark could omit the eunuch statement because at the time he wrote his gospel, it was the norm for the divorced person to marry again, and divorced people understood this. Mark would not include the eunuch statement because there was *no need to state the obvious*—of course the divorced will marry again if there is sexual attraction. Since this was not a change in any way, it was not necessary to relate.

Picture the scene: The disciples exclaim, "It is better not to marry?!" Jesus answers the obvious, "Only if you're a eunuch." The disciples slap their forehead and laugh. Conversation over.

Further, if this is Jesus' answer to the disciples, then it is also his answer to us. No, for most, it is *not better to avoid remarriage* after divorce! It is not better!

Although we might accurately understand Jesus' words in Matthew 5:17-48 at the Sermon on the Mount, and although we might thoroughly understand that in 5:31-32 Jesus was not giving instructions about remarriage after divorce, we can easily fall into the mindset, "Well, if it's adultery, it would be *better* not to remarry." No! We must not fool ourselves. For most it is not better "not to marry," and *Jesus himself* tells us so!

Thankfully, for the church today, Matthew did include the eunuch statement—because of various traditions in the church, we do need the obvious stated. With Matthew's inclusion of the eunuch statement, the divorced can know, and the church can know, that the divorced have Jesus' approval to marry again.

---

[38] In personal matters, church leaders do not have such authority over us. They do not have authority to tell us where to live, where to work, if we should marry, who to marry, or if we should divorce. (This is in contrast to cults where the leaders do exercise such authority.)

A Practical Application

We might ask, "What does this mean for me?" For those who have been living under a burden of other people's rules and expectations, and not just in respect to divorce, the Matthew 19/Mark 10 passage is good news.

The Bible is a gift and a treasure, and we must allow it to transform us. We often say the Bible is our guide, maybe quoting verses that have helped on our journey. True, but the Bible is more than that—God reveals himself to us through his Word; every page reveals who He is. The more time we spend in the Word, the more our thinking and understanding are guided into correct paths.

If we neglect the Word, we will become either someone whose decisions are shaped by his or her own human understanding or someone who is burdened under the rules and expectations of others. It is the daily transformation of the Word of God and the leading of the Holy Spirit that guides us and protects us from going in either of these God-ignoring directions.

10 | Jesus' Fourth Mention of Divorce

Jesus mentions divorce on four occasions. We dealt with the first in Part I and the second and third in the prior chapters of Part II. This last chapter of Part II considers the fourth occasion, which is found in Luke 16:18. We cover it in its own chapter because Scripture presents it separately from the other three. In fact, Luke includes it as part of three statements about the law (these verses can be read in their context in Appendix F).

The first statement in this passage about the law was directed toward the Pharisees. The immediate context is the Pharisees had mocked Jesus after he told the parable of the steward who had squandered the possessions of his master and was called to account (Luke 16:1-8). After that parable, Jesus made additional comments about money and possessions (Luke 16:9-13), which riled the Pharisees. This led to Jesus' first statement about the law.

The Pharisees, who were lovers of money, heard all these things, and they ridiculed him. And he said to them, "You are those who justify yourselves before men, but God knows your hearts. For what is exalted among men is an abomination in the sight of God. The Law and the Prophets were until John; since then the good news of the kingdom of God is preached, and everyone forces his way into it. (Luke 16:14-15 ESV)

The Pharisees initiated this conversation by ridiculing Jesus. We do not know what form the ridicule took, but by it they gave Jesus an opportunity to publicize that they justify themselves in the sight of men. Jesus used it as a springboard to correct and rebuke the Pharisees' thinking and behavior.

Jesus' words "You are those who justify yourselves before men" reveals at least two shortcomings in the Pharisaic system. One is that men set the standards for what is acceptable to God. As the religious authorities of the day, the Pharisees had developed an intricate set of rules for what was religiously acceptable. A significant problem with this approach is that it is impossible for humans to comprehend God's standards for righteousness (much less fulfill them), so it is an understatement to say that humans should not establish the rules for what is acceptable to God.

The other shortcoming is that not only were mere humans (Pharisees) creating the rules, but they also wanted other mere humans to approve of their righteousness (all who would be watching them). Of course it is foolish and shortsighted to seek the justification of men; it should be God's justification we seek.

Jesus implies the Pharisees' behavior is an abomination to God. Abomination seems to be a harsh word because it is not as though the Pharisees did things we would normally consider to be abominable.[39] Most of the things they did would seem to an impartial observer as perhaps dedicated, possibly eccentric, tedious, interfering, or bothersome, and maybe selfish as in their love of money, but this behavior would not typically be called abominable. Nevertheless, an abomination is how God saw their behavior, and it is how God sees the behavior of any of us who rely on our own righteousness. Our best efforts, accomplished by our own strength, are in God's sight, completely unacceptable. As Isaiah says, "All our righteousness is as filthy rags." This is such a core element to the Gospel, and it is what sinners find such a relief to acknowledge!

In Jesus' second statement about the law, he turns the conversation away from the Pharisees' self-righteousness and towards the good news of the kingdom of God. Here, it is not clear

---

[39] The Greek word Jesus used is *bdeluktos*. BDAG gives the meaning of this word as "something disgusting that arouses wrath" or "something that is totally defiling, abomination, pollutant." Walter Bauer, *A Greek-English Lexicon of the New Testament and Other Early Christian Literature, 3rd ed.* Revised and Edited by Frederick William Danker. (BDAG) (Chicago: The University of Chicago Press, 2000), 172

to whom Jesus is speaking, but he was likely speaking to all who would listen.[40]

> *The Law and the Prophets were until John; since then the good news of the kingdom of God is preached, and everyone forces his way into it.*   (Luke 16:16 ESV)

Initially, the Law and the Prophets foretold Jesus' coming. Then, John heralded the arrival of Jesus. Finally, Jesus himself was in the world, and he began to preach the gospel—the good news of our salvation. The Pharisees missed it while others were crowding Jesus and following him and staying with him for days as they wanted to hear more of this new teaching. The Pharisees desired to be admired and honored by the crowds, but instead, it was Jesus whose popularity was growing, and it was Jesus who the crowds followed. People were forcing their way to hear what Jesus was saying and doing. This is the very thing the Pharisees were trying to stop.

Last, we come to Jesus' third statement.

> *But it is easier for heaven and earth to pass away than for one dot of the Law to become void.*
> *Everyone who divorces his wife and marries another commits adultery, and he who marries a woman divorced from her husband commits adultery.*
>
> (Luke 16:17-18 ESV)

This statement likely reminded the listeners of Jesus' Matthew 5:17-48 sermon. Notice how the above two verses repeat Jesus' words from his Matthew 5:17-48 salvation message,

> *For truly, I say to you, until heaven and earth pass away, not an iota, not a dot, will pass from the Law until all is accomplished.*
> *Everyone who divorces his wife (besides for immorality) makes her to commit adultery, and whoever marries a divorced woman commits adultery.*   (Matthew 5:18, 32)

---

[40] The lack of clarity is demonstrated in that various translations differ in how they group the verses in Luke 16.

Here, in Luke 16:17-18, Jesus very briefly condenses and reiterates his Matthew 5:17-48 teaching. The point is, the entire law must be fulfilled, and complete righteousness is necessary according to God's holy standard.

To summarize all three statements, we see that justifying ourselves and being thought of as righteous by others are completely the opposite of what our goal should be; instead, our desire should be to be declared righteous by God. Many of us seem to innately realize we need a righteousness that is acceptable before God, and many of us have lived under the burden of trying to earn that righteousness through our own efforts to be good or keep the law or other rules. Yet all *our* efforts to be good or to be righteous fall short and are even an abomination in the sight of God.

There is only one way to obtain that righteousness—through Jesus. By perfectly fulfilling righteousness for us, Jesus freed us from that burden. This is the Good News.

Finally, notice that this divorce statement in Luke contains no *parektos* clause or *mē epi* clause; there is no clause at all. It is a blunt statement—all marriage by a divorced person or to a divorced person is adultery. If this blunt statement had triggered questions or caused any confusion, the answer could be found in Matthew 5:17-48 and in Jesus' eunuch statement in Matthew 19:11-12.

We have now, in Parts I and II, covered everything Jesus said about divorce. Next, in Parts III and IV, we move on to examine what Paul says.

PART III

Divorce and Domestic Abuse— God Is Not Silent

11 | What Is Abuse?
What Does Scripture Say About Abuse?

We will examine three of Paul's comments about marriage and divorce. Two of the better known comments are in 1 Corinthians 7,[41] but before we proceed to these (in Part IV), we will follow Paul's sequence and consider first his words in 1 Corinthians 5 and 6 where he mentions abuse and gives relevant instructions. A discussion about domestic abuse is included because this is one of the main reasons why a woman might seek a divorce.

Many Christians have wondered why the Bible does not seem to speak about the issue of abuse in marriage; the apparent silence of the Bible almost makes it seem as if abuse does not matter to God. But how could demeaning verbal attacks, taunts, threats to kill the wife, choking, and other abuses too horrible to mention, even to the point of murder, not matter to God?

Up until the recent past, the opinion of many of our church leaders was that the wife must put up with such a man and she should pray to God for help to bear the abuse. They believe this because they think the Bible 1) is silent about abuse, and 2) says a wife should not separate from her husband or divorce an abuser who claims to be a believer. This may sound calloused, but there are still some today who hold the conviction that this is what Scripture teaches.

Persuaded perhaps by more recent cultural influence, many of our church leaders have adopted a somewhat fragmented view; they

---

[41] 1 Corinthians 7:10b-11a, "A wife must not separate from her husband. But if she does, she must remain unmarried." And 1 Corinthians 7:13, "And if a woman has a husband who is not a believer and he is willing to live with her, she must not divorce him." (NIV)

permit abused women to legally separate from their husbands, but insist the wives must not divorce their abusive husbands.

Still others, focusing on the kindness and compassion of God, say these women should be freed from their abusive husbands. They allow, and even encourage, these women to free themselves and divorce their husbands even though they have difficulty supporting this view from the Bible.

For the most part, the church has stumbled around in our thinking about abuse, not educating ourselves about the nature of abuse and missing Scriptural answers. Yet we are willing to force life-changing decisions on women, or in the case of some women, life-ending decisions.

Much of this confusion comes because we think the Bible does not speak about abuse, but in fact, it does. Although Scripture clearly addresses abuse, this may be a new thought to many Bible students.

We will address two basic reasons for the prevalent thinking that the Bible does not speak about this subject. The first is because most of us do not have a clear idea of what abuse is, and the second is we do not recognize the places where the Bible describes abuse.[42]

What Is Abuse?
Four Common Types of Abuse

We begin by discussing the nature of abuse so that we may better understand what it really is and expose misunderstandings about it. Then we will be better able to recognize it in Scripture. Most of us think domestic abuse is physical; that is, we define abuse as, for example, a husband choking his wife or slamming her against

---

[42] In this book, we focus on abuse of husbands towards their wives. Around the world, the overwhelming burden of partner violence is born by women at the hands of men. Only 8% reported abuse is females towards males, and this 8% includes women who were responding to abuse by the male. Barbara Roberts, *Not Under Bondage: Biblical Divorce for Abuse, Adultery & Desertion* (Maschil Press, 2008), 19

the wall, punching her, and other physical assaults that are difficult to even think about. These are obviously abusive.

Many of us, however, do not understand that a husband can abuse his wife even if he does not lay a hand on her. There are many types of abuse besides the physical abuse just mentioned, such as verbal, psychological, spiritual, sexual, relational, or financial. We will give a few examples of how abuse can look.

A husband might abuse his wife by going into a rage, shouting, throwing and breaking things, cursing, insulting, taunting, and even threatening to kill his wife with the purpose of intimidating her and terrifying her. In all of this, he might not lay a hand on her.

The husband could employ a constant and more subtle method of abuse. For example, he can verbally abuse his wife *without even raising his voice*; but instead, in a measured and calculated tone, insult, demean, taunt, mock, make unreasonable demands, threaten and terrify her, and express irritation, disgust, and disapproval. He might, for days on end, badger her about some issue, or multiple issues, and no amount of submission or agreement on the wife's part will bring the badgering to an end. The badgering ends when the husband decides it will end and not a moment sooner.

A husband might abuse his wife through extremely controlling measures. For example, he might lock her out of the house. He might lock her in the bathroom. He might leave her and the children stranded somewhere. He might keep all the money under his control and make her beg when she needs something. He might throw into the garbage a meal she has prepared. He might destroy her personal possessions. He might isolate her from her friends and family.

In addition, alcohol may be present in any of the above situations and might confuse the abuse issue for the wife. However, alcohol acts as a depressant, and as such, does not directly make people belligerent, aggressive, or violent. In *Why Does He Do That*, Lundy Bancroft explains that alcohol contributes to partner abuse in two common ways. One, if the man *believes* it can make him aggressive, he may act on that belief, and two, the man can use it as a convenient excuse for his abusive behavior ("Sorry about last night, I was really trashed").[43]

We should understand that even in situations that might not seem to us to be physically dangerous, a wife could still be abused, intimidated, threatened, and demeaned. Even the subtle methods are insidious and pervasive. With the subtle methods, the husband conveys the warning that if the wife should venture a thought, a plan, a desire, or an action other than what meets his approval, it might trigger one of his bouts of belittlement, or he might tighten his controlling measures, or he might set off on one of his rages. Without question, the more subtle methods are also abuse and often intentionally carry the threat of physical assault or a rage.

With all these methods, the husband controls the wife. In fact, abuse is all about control and the rush of power he feels from controlling and demeaning her.[44] He is like the neighborhood bully who gets a perverted pleasure from tormenting someone's pet cat. The husband may not need to use physical abuse or rages because his more cunning words and methods control her while at the same time satisfy his sick heart. Yet, physical abuse and rages are also methods he can use when either he lets his evil heart go or when he finds it necessary to bring his wife back under sufficient fear, to remind the wife he is the one who controls everything. The wife learns to do what he says, she learns not to offer an opinion, not to mention her own point of view, and eventually, if she stays long enough, she learns not even to have an opinion or a point of view of her own.

People typically advise wives to strive to figure out what are the triggers that might set off the abuse and then attempt to avoid them, but this effort will not help; in fact, it reveals a fundamental lack of understanding of the cause of abuse. An abusive husband desires to keep his wife under his control, and he finds a perverse pleasure in keeping her in a state of fear and tension. In fact, he prefers her to be in a state of tension, and to do so, he will

---

[43] Lundy Bancroft, *Why Does He Do That? Inside the Minds of Angry and Controlling Men* (New York: Berkley Books, 2002), 200-201
[44] Ibid. 152-153

continually adopt new triggers. He keeps his wife in a constant state of anxiety; she walks on eggshells at all times. Distressingly, for these women, this evil permeates all of their waking and sleeping moments.

Another common assumption is the abusive husband has an anger or temper problem that simply needs to be controlled, but this is a seriously inadequate view of abuse, and in fact, advice offered from this uninformed view is likely to worsen the situation. Unless and until we have a good grasp of the nature of abuse, we should be very careful about the advice or counsel we give to the woman or man involved.

We have only touched on a few issues regarding the nature of abuse but will end this part of the abuse overview because more is beyond the scope of this book. If you are involved with an abusive person or situation, we strongly encourage you to read one or more of the excellent books on the subject listed in Appendix E, which also lists ways to obtain immediate help.

What Does Scripture Say About Abuse?

When we understand the nature of abuse, we see it is right to call it evil. Most of us have never noticed the Apostle Paul also calls it evil. He says,

I wrote to you in my letter not to associate with sexually immoral people—not at all meaning the sexually immoral of this world, or the greedy and swindlers, or idolaters, since then you would need to go out of the world. But now I am writing to you not to associate with anyone who bears the name of brother if he is guilty of sexual immorality or greed, or is an idolater, reviler, drunkard, or swindler—not even to eat with such a one. For what have I to do with judging outsiders? Is it not those inside the church whom you are to judge? God judges those outside. "Purge the evil person from among you."   (1 Corinthians 5:9-13)

Did you see it? Most people miss it. That is because we do not know what the word revile means. It seems a rather old-fashioned word to us; we read it but skip past it without a second thought. The noun in the Greek is *loidoros*; it is used twice in the Greek New Testament. The Greek lexicon gives the definition of *loidoros* as: [45]

- A reviler
- An abusive person

Since most of us are not entirely familiar with what the English word revile means, here is the definition[46]:

- To subject to verbal abuse
- To use abusive language
- To attack with abusive language

Combining the Greek and English definitions, we see that a *loidoros* is an abusive person or a verbally abusive person, with somewhat more emphasis on the verbal abuse. Notice that a person who is verbally abusive, but never physically abusive, meets the definition of a *loidoros*.

What does Paul say about this person who calls himself a brother?

- Do not associate with this person.
- Do not eat with this person.
- This behavior is evil.
- Purge (expel or remove) the evil person from among you.

For a start, we see that 1 Corinthians 5 absolutely does address the abusive husband, and we can draw four important conclusions:

1. This Scripture identifies the abuser and addresses him severely.

---

[45] Walter Bauer, *A Greek-English Lexicon of the New Testament and Other Early Christian Literature, 3rd ed.* Revised and Edited by Frederick William Danker. (BDAG) (Chicago: The University of Chicago Press, 2000), s.v. "*loidoros*."
[46] http://www.merriam-webster.com/dictionary/revile
http://www.yourdictionary.com/revile Accessed July 12, 2016

2. We see that even verbal abuse (to say nothing of physical abuse) is recognized as evil.

3. We are not to associate with the abuser.

4. He is to be expelled from among us.

We all have known people who fall into the category of *loidoros*; for example, a demeaning boss, a demanding co-worker, a ranting coach, an intolerant neighbor, or a jealous acquaintance who attacks with false accusations. However, there are very few people who would be an example of a worse *loidoros* than an abusive husband.[47]

Paul wrote this letter to the individual members of the church in Corinth. The questions for the members of the Corinthian church and for the members of our churches today would be, "Are we willing to stop associating with this person? Will we refuse to eat with this person? Do we have the backbone to call this evil? Will we be obedient and purge this person from among us?"

Church members do not have to wait for their pastor or elders to take these actions; Paul wrote these things to the individual members of the church and fully expected them to act on his words. We should consider this a call to both individual members and to church leaders to do so and together send a consistent message to the abuser.

As we continue our study about domestic abuse, we will see in Chapter 12 that Paul has additional serious words to say about the spiritual condition of a *loidoros*, and in Chapter 13, we will learn more about Paul's command, "Purge the evil from among you."

---

[47] We can see that this Scriptural definition of abuse can also describe a wife. She can be abusive to her husband with cruel, manipulative, or cutting words, subtly demeaning him and deviously attempting to control him. She can also fly into a rage in an effort to control him, and in some instances be physically abusive.

12 | Is Church Discipline Appropriate? Looking at Biblical Repentance

How do we respond when an abuser claims to be saved? We have already seen that Paul says such a man should be purged or expelled from the church. Does that mean this man is not a believer? How should we consider this man spiritually? How did Paul consider the abusive man? What if the abuser repents? Repentance is always a good thing; yet, what is the repentance that is appropriate and needed from a *loidoros*? And what if others do not see him as a bad guy? A lot of questions arise—keep reading for some Scriptural responses.

What Is the Spiritual Condition of the Abuser?

Paul tells us,

Do you not know that the unrighteous will not inherit the kingdom of God? Do not be deceived: neither the sexually immoral, nor idolaters, nor adulterers, nor men who practice homosexuality, nor thieves, nor the greedy, nor drunkards, nor revilers, nor swindlers will inherit the kingdom of God. And such were some of you. But you were washed, you were sanctified, you were justified in the name of the Lord Jesus Christ and by the Spirit of our God.

(1 Corinthians 6:9-11)

The people mentioned in this list are people whose lives are characterized by the described behavior, and we again see reviler or *loidoros*. Paul clearly states, "Do not be deceived, revilers will not inherit the kingdom of God." In other words, a *loidoros* is not saved. Revilers are not saved. Can Paul be any more direct, any clearer? He even says, "Do not be deceived." Do not be deceived—revilers are not saved. Have we been deceived?

What About Church Discipline?

Some people think church discipline is in order and want to apply the steps of Matthew 18:15-20. However, because this man is not saved, by definition, he is not part of the church; therefore, these steps do not apply. In fact, Paul has already made a judgment and pronounced a sentence for us. Paul helps us make this judgment when he says,

For though absent in body, I am present in spirit; and as if present, I have already pronounced judgment on the one who did such a thing. When you are assembled in the name of the Lord Jesus and my spirit is present, with the power of our Lord Jesus, you are to deliver this man to Satan for the destruction of the flesh, so that his spirit may be saved in the day of the Lord.

(1 Corinthians 5:3-5)

It seems as if Paul understands that dealing with an abuser (or anyone in the 1 Corinthians 5:9-13; 6:9-11 list) will be difficult for us. No one wants to believe that someone who has presented himself as a brother and has been active in a local church and treated as a brother, is not saved. It is not always clear cut, and our compassionate side wants to keep reaching out.

It can be uncomfortable, difficult, and messy to make someone leave the church, and we tend not to want to do it. Paul foresees the difficulty, first by making the decision for us, and then by taking the burden off our shoulders telling us that it is as if Paul "were present" and that he has "already pronounced judgment." In other words, when the church confronts an abuser, they can respond with the confidence they would have if Paul were present himself and had already passed judgment for them. [48]

Once the church has determined the husband is an abuser, Paul tells us what to think—do not be deceived; he is not saved. Paul tells

---

[48] We need not get side-tracked about the phrase "deliver this man to Satan" in verse 5; the phrase might refer to the steps Paul describes.

us what to do—do not eat with him, do not associate with him, and purge him from among us.

The church must take this matter seriously. We may think we do, but seldom are we as serious about this as Paul. We give the abuser every chance, we send the couple to counseling, we send the husband to anger-management classes, we set him up with accountability partners, we fight the breakup of a marriage with every fiber of our being—but this was not Paul's attitude about the situation or his instructions to us. Paul gives the abuser no second chance; he kicks the abusive husband out of the church and forbids us to associate with him. Paul instructs a complete separation. Are we this serious?[49] Of course, kicking someone out of the church is a serious step. However, allowing an abuser to remain in the church is just as serious, if not more so.

Finally, we must make a distinction between the decision to kick someone out of the church and the decision to divorce. The church makes the decision to expel someone; the woman decides about divorce as led by the Holy Spirit.

What If the Abuser Claims to Have Repented?

If an abuser is truly repentant and not merely continuing his attempts to deceive, what should we expect to see? The repentance needed from an abuser should include his admission that he is not saved. Yet many revilers will not admit they are revilers and will not admit they are unsaved.

It is to our shame when revilers are helped along this road of denial by the church when it refuses to call such a man a *loidoros*, refuses to call his behavior evil, refuses to call this person unsaved, and refuses to purge such a person from the church. Paul warns us and makes it clear. He says, "*Do not be deceived*; a *loidoros* will not inherit the kingdom of God." Paul knows it is likely we would be

---

[49] We may face circumstances that call for wisdom in applying this command, especially if life brings us in close contact with a *loidoros* who calls himself a brother; e.g., a coworker, boss, or relative. Each believer works this out as he or she applies these instructions in the Word as guided by the Holy Spirit.

deceived in this area. We like to think the best of people, but Paul says this man is not saved. He is not a Christian.

Stop for a moment and consider the consequences of encouraging this man to think of himself as a believer when he is not. He may think all his conflicted thoughts and confusion are typical of Christians; he may even express occasional doubts over whether he is saved. No thanks to most people in the church, he has no idea that what he needs is a new heart because we are rarely willing to tell him the truth. The Holy Spirit may be convicting an abuser of the need to be saved, but he can barely hear the Spirit because our voices are so loud as we agree with him that he is a Christian (or as we counsel him that he can have "assurance of his salvation"). He will likely end up in hell, yet it is the very ones who should be confronting him of his need to be saved who nudged and pushed him there.

We do no favor for a *loidoros* by soft-pedaling his sin, and we do him no favor by agreeing with him when he says he is saved when the evidence of his behavior points against it. Scripture itself says the abusive husband is not saved. If this man wants to repent, he should have an uncompromising confession that he is repenting from abuse and that he is not saved. Then, praise God, he can be justified and sanctified in the name of the Lord Jesus Christ and by the Spirit of God.

What If the Abuser Expresses Remorse? Or Asks for Forgiveness?

It is common for abusers to feel some kind of remorse after the wife leaves. He tells her he has repented, and he may even believe it; after all, when she is not in front of him and he is not abusing her, he may think he has changed. He may even ask for forgiveness (abusers do have temporary changes in attitude), and she may return and give him another try. Things are fine for a short time, but soon the abuse resumes.

Studies show that an abused woman will go back an average of five times before she finally leaves for good.[50] Yet very few abusers ever change.[51] We should fully understand and acknowledge this is the situation—that abusers rarely change—and help the woman not go back, not even a second time. No one should urge the wife to return and become the husband's (and the church's) guinea pig, to be the guinea pig that tests this man to see if his words of repentance are real and lasting; they seldom are. Forgiveness by the wife does not obligate her to return to the abuser!

For a *loidoros*, for an abusive husband, abuse and deception are the essence of who he is because abuse and deception come from his heart. An unsaved heart drives him, and one way it manifests itself is with abuse. This is a matter of an unsaved heart that is separated from Christ. In order for an abuser to truly repent, he must confess he is a *loidoros* and that a *loidoros* is not saved. He must be saved, and his repentance must show fruit.

A common mistake in repentance is the person repents of just that *one* besetting sin (whatever it might be) and hopes God will remove that one sin. However, when a person turns to Christ, he or she must give up his or her whole life; every part must be given to Christ to be made new. The *loidoros* must turn his whole life over to Christ, not just the abuse. This is hard to do; it is impossible without God. But we make it even harder if the church does not communicate truth to him and sends him mixed messages.

What Does True Repentance Look Like?

When a *loidoros* becomes saved, his fruit of repentance should be obvious to all. For example, he should confess to the local church fellowship that he was not saved before and that he was an abuser. He should admit that he abused his wife without blaming her for any of his behavior. He should allow the woman to express any

---

[50] Elaine Weiss, Ed.D., *Family and Friends' Guide to Domestic Violence: How to Listen, Talk and Take Action When Someone You Care About is Being Abused* (Volcano, California: Volcano Press, 2003), 125

[51] Lundy Bancroft, *Why Does He Do That? Inside the Minds of Angry and Controlling Men* (New York: Berkley Books, 2002), 335

thoughts, feelings, and opinions to him that she has had to keep closed up for months or years (if she cares to). He should do whatever possible to vindicate and clear the woman's name. An example of this might be repaying the costs his former wife has incurred because of his abuse (hospital costs, counseling costs, shelter and housing costs, moving expenses, divorce expenses, costs incurred to start a new life on her own). The members of the church, who may know other details, might expect further fruit of repentance, which a truly repentant man would be willing to do. Actions that have a personal cost may reflect true repentance and a heart made new by the Lord Jesus.

Actions of the unrepentant abuser that fall short of the above description can easily be mistaken for the fruit of repentance, and often are, but we should not be fooled by superficial acts that indicate a lack of true repentance. Actions that serve his purposes should not be considered true repentance. If we come away from a "repentance" conversation thinking better of him and worse of her—especially if we also have feelings of pity for him, or if he is seen as a "hero" for wanting to keep the marriage going, we are likely deceived (this man's actions destroyed the marriage). He may play on the sympathy of others—"I'm so sorry how I treated her" or "I've changed!" or "I love her so much and miss her and the children." Beware of tears and flowery language about his marriage or his wife if not accompanied by actions reflecting true repentance.

Some examples that should not be mistaken for repentance follow:

- He makes comments like, "I lost my temper" or "I treated her inappropriately" or "Maybe I shouldn't have done this, but *she* did such and such." (He excuses and minimizes his behavior and avoids calling it what it is—abuse. If he cannot name his sin, how can he repent of it?)

- He is active in church. (This allows him to feel good about himself. It also lets others react positively toward him, thus fueling his good feelings. Church activity sidetracks him from addressing his true need).

- He wants to "pour out his heart" to his wife or her family or friends. (This makes him feel good about himself and possibly makes him look good to others, but it does nothing for the wife or his lost soul.)

- He agrees to go to anger management classes. (Abuse is not an anger issue and displaying anger is just *one* of his many methods of control; again, a distraction from his real need and his core issue).

What If No One Else Sees Him as a Bad Guy?

There is another reality of domestic abuse we must mention as we consider genuine repentance. The *loidoros* husband aims his abuse at his wife behind closed doors, but he often fools most other people as he feigns an amiable or reasonable personality. We should realize that without true repentance, any good behavior is an act or is accomplished by sheer willpower. When the abusive husband is around others, he relies on willpower with quite good success because his good behavior is necessary only for short periods of time. When he is with his wife, he gives way to his evil heart. An abuser of those in the home is also a manipulator of those outside the home.

We must be on our guard against, and even expect, attempts to deceive with false expressions of repentance—these are very common. The effective ability of abusers to deceive is one important reason why church leaders and church members should be educated about this aspect of the abusive husband so they can avoid being taken in by this good behavior.

13 | What About Legal Separation?
What If He Wants to Stay Married?
What If the Abuse Is Not Physical?

The abused woman faces many challenges when she takes steps to get out of her situation. In this chapter we discuss three issues she is likely to encounter when she is considering her options. Often they are brought up as more than issues to consider and may be presented as objections to divorce. We show they are not biblical or valid arguments.

Legal Separation

There are many in the church who do not expect a woman to stay with the abusive husband, but they also will not admit or recognize that divorce is allowed. They insist the only solution is a legal separation. However, as we have just learned in Jesus' confrontation with the Pharisees, other people were never authorized by Scripture to make pronouncements in the matter. It is up to the woman in the abusive marriage to make her own decisions as Scripture and the Holy Spirit guide her.

An abused woman likely will have heard about legal separations and wondered if that would be the best step for her. There are considerations an abused woman should take into account. First, although a couple with a legal separation is still married, the issues addressed in a divorce are also addressed in a legal separation, and a legal separation is granted by a court just as is a divorce decree. So this route will not let a woman avoid the court system or a legal decree.

Second, there seems to be no basis in Scripture for the idea of a legal separation, and accordingly, those who insist that the acceptable Christian action is a legal separation instead of a divorce have gone beyond Scripture with this rule.[52] A legal separation may seem to be satisfactory and righteous, but if used simply for the purpose of avoiding divorce, it is more of a Pharisaic approach to the issue.[53]

Third, simply because the Bible is silent about legal separations, it is not necessarily ruled out as an option. There are many topics not mentioned in the Bible in which we have freedom to make choices and decisions. But again, it would be the woman in the abusive situation who would make the decision about a legal separation.

Finally, this being said, a legal separation does not seem to be consistent with Paul's commands. In 1 Corinthians 5:13, we are commanded, "Purge the evil from among you." This command is a reference to several Old Testament verses that describe people who had sinned in various and specific ways, and the Israelites were commanded to purge the evil from among them.[54]

It is key to our discussion to identify the method the Israelites used to purge the evil. In all but one of these references, they were to purge the evil by putting the sinner to death. Death was the main method of purging the evil in the Old Testament. We, of course, would not put such a person to death—that was the sentence in the theocratic nation of Israel, but the severity of the punishment shown in Old Testament passages can guide us in understanding the gravity of the sin and the seriousness of the instruction to the church.

Paul still requires we expel the evil person from our group, and because of its Old Testament use, we can recognize that this means more than just tell someone not to be a part of our group. When Paul says not to associate with such a person, not even to eat with such a person, and to purge the person from among us, we should recognize

---

[52] Sometimes I Corinthians 7:10-11 is mistakenly understood to support separation instead of divorce. We will deal with this in Chapter 18.
[53] Some countries in the world require a legal separation before a divorce is permitted, which is a different situation than what is discussed in this section.
[54] Deuteronomy 13:5, 17:7, 17:12, 19:19, 21:21, 22:21-22, 22:24, and 24:7.

these actions are the New Testament equivalent of considering the person to be as separate from us as one who has been put to death.

Scripture makes it clear that it is not our job to maintain a relationship with an abuser even with the goal of bringing him to repentance. The abuser has been in the church and has heard the gospel.

Does this sound harsh? Let us review what Paul says about a *loidoros* who claims to be a brother:

- He is not saved (he will not inherit the Kingdom of God).
- Do not associate with him.
- Do not eat with him.
- This is evil.
- Purge the evil person from among you.

Consider these from the wife's point of view. These commands, and the pronouncement that this person is evil, are highly significant and fundamental to how the abused wife should consider her situation. The complete and drastic separation brought about by purging the evil clearly allows, and may even suggest or favor, divorce.

Consider these from the church's point of view. Paul commands us to expel the man from the church and he commands us what our *individual* actions must be, but the church does not make the decision for the woman (the woman is the one who makes her own decision in her own individual situation).

He Wants to Remain Married

A second issue is when the abuser says he wants to stay married. Some in the church then say the wife must not divorce him. They think Paul's words in 1 Corinthians 7 say this,

If any woman has a husband who is an unbeliever, and he consents to live with her, she should not divorce him.

(1 Corinthians 7:13)

The key phrase in 1 Corinthians 7:13, is "consents to live with her." In the Greek, "consents to live with" is *suneudokeō* and literally means "together thinks it is good." It has the idea that the people involved agree together about something or approve of something together, that they have a mutual agreement.

In the Greek New Testament, this mutual agreement is not limited to a good purpose only but can also be mutual consent for any purpose. For example, in Acts 7:54-8:1, when we read that the men who were stoning Stephen were laying their coats by the feet of a young man named Saul, we see in 8:1 that "Saul was there, consenting to his death." Consenting is the word *suneudokeō*. Paul agreed with the men stoning Stephen—they all agreed that stoning Stephen was a good thing. This example demonstrates that the point of the word is a mutual agreement and that the parties are "on the same page."

Therefore, in 1 Corinthians 7:13, the unbeliever who wants to stay with the believing spouse, by definition, has a mutual-agreement attitude with the believing spouse, agrees to the implications of being married to a believer, and consents to live with a spouse who acts on those beliefs. He or she makes a choice that allows the believing spouse to live as a Christian and to express his or her life as a practicing Christian.

This, of course, would not be the case with an abusive husband. He rarely tolerates his wife having opinions of her own nor would she be allowed to express her Christian life in the way a Christian should and would desire. When Paul says an unbelieving husband "consents to live with her," he is not referring to the abusive husband who wants to remain married. We know Paul is *not* referring to an abusive husband because mutual agreement is not a part of an abusive marriage.

1 Corinthians 7:13 does not apply to an abusive marriage. Instead, it refers to a man who is sympathetic to and willing to be married to a practicing Christian wife and to be married in the accepted and true sense of the word. This does not describe an abusive husband. Understanding the meaning of *suneudokeō* and the

nature of abuse will help the church and the woman in an abusive marriage have an accurate view about her situation. [55]

We must also consider the mindset of the abusive husband. For various reasons, he seldom files for divorce. If he is in Christian circles, he may think if the wife is the petitioner, he can blame her. He can say that she is the one who filed for the divorce and she is the one who ended the marriage. He has a goal of maintaining his reputation among Christian circles, and he thinks he can do this by not being the petitioner. Hopefully, we all see this for the hypocrisy it is and that it is a manipulative, face-saving maneuver.

Another reason the abusive husband may not want a divorce is because the abusive relationship satisfies his sick heart. He considers his wife as his property, someone to abuse and control, and he does not want to give up his property. She is the convenient outlet for his evil passions, and he may not give that up easily.

When the abuser says he wants to remain married, it is not marriage in any accepted and true sense of the word that he envisions or desires. He has shown by his actions that the true meaning of marriage is not a part of his thinking.

When the Abuse Is Not Physical

The third issue is that many women find themselves in a verbally abusive marriage but not in a physically abusive marriage. How does all of this apply to them? For the answer to this, we go back to the meaning of the word *loidoros*—a *loidoros* is an abusive person or a verbally abusive person, with somewhat more emphasis on the verbal abuse than the physical abuse. So yes, this word applies to the woman who is in a verbally abusive marriage but not a physically abusive marriage. The church is still commanded to purge the verbally abusive husband from among themselves.

---

[55] We will discuss *suneudokeō* again in Chapter 19 and discover how it should be applied in other marriage situations.

14 | How the Local Congregation Should Relate to the Woman

Facing abuse and going through separation or divorce is an incredibly confusing time for the wife. Consider all the things she has to process: the abuse, that her husband is not who she thought he was, the loss of her dreams, an uncertain future, the ramifications for her children.

For a Christian woman there are additional issues. She may want to leave her abusive situation, yet she may find that her greatest difficulty is facing an often ignorant, unhelpful, and antagonistic church. She may feel she cannot even consider divorce because she is told that divorce is wrong, but then what does that mean for her future?

While in the process of coming to grips with her situation or even after these women finally break free from their abuser, they often spend hours trying to elicit support and help from their church leaders and church members. They end up having to reveal intimate details of their marriage only to find that many of these people continue to think the husband was simply losing his temper and that counseling and anger-management classes are the answer. The wife often encounters skepticism, criticism, or condemnation when she attempts to make her plight known to the local fellowship. She cannot convince the church leaders that her husband is an abuser and that his evil has been aimed directly at her! Be aware—abusers get a depraved satisfaction from watching the wife face disbelief or blame from these leaders. We should be on guard against unwittingly participating in the husband's "game."

Brothers and sisters can also unknowingly add to the woman's hurt and pain. Imagine how disheartening it is for an abused woman when she hears, "We hope you don't feel bad and we hope you understand that we are still friends with _____ (the abusive husband)." But what did Paul say? He said, "Do not eat with him, do not associate with him, purge this man from among you." Aside from showing compassion to the woman, it would also be helpful to the man if everyone would send him a consistent message.

The church does not show love, insight, concern, or care when it insists a woman stay in a dangerous situation. This is presumptuous and a careless way to treat life, and the abused woman need not bow to that pressure.

The woman in an abusive situation should know the Apostle Paul supports her, but she will need others to help and encourage her. Some help is out there, but sadly, for many, the church is not the place to find that help. Regrettably, many women have found more support and understanding outside the church.

However, the church can change. The church can adopt Paul's assessment of the situation that the abuser is not saved, that his behavior is evil, that we should not associate or even eat with the abuser, and that we should expel the abuser from us.

A church can have as part of its mission statement that it will fully support any abused spouse. The statement could say something such as, "Because Paul commands the church to make a complete separation, we will fully support the divorce of an abused wife, even paying some of her expenses if necessary. We will help vindicate her name to everyone who knows about the divorce and make it clear that the abusive husband is responsible for the destruction of the marriage and the subsequent divorce."

Churches should make sure that all those in leadership positions as well as all individual members of the church are fully informed and fully understand the nature of abusive situations; they will then have the background and tools required to recognize and identify an abusive situation, and they will know not to ask for unnecessary personal details. Anyone who is not fully informed and does not fully understand the nature of abuse should not offer an opinion and definitely should not counsel any abused woman. Not only is this hurtful to the abused woman, but it can literally be a matter of life and death.

Summary

The purpose of Part III is to provide clarity and encouragement about what the Bible says concerning abuse in marriage.

It provides clarity for the wife by demonstrating that the Bible:

- does not say she needs to attempt to salvage the marriage.

- encourages her that this is not her fault, but rather her husband's.

- does not suggest she wait for the approval of others to make her decision (although she may choose to do so).

It provides clarity for the church by demonstrating that the Bible:

- does not say the marriage needs to be salvaged.

- encourages believers that the appropriate response toward the wife is to recognize that she has been married to a *loidoros*.

- lays out that the biblical response and attitude of believers towards the *loidoros* is to acknowledge his behavior is evil, to purge him from the church, and to refrain from associating with him.

- does not give us permission to pressure her to return to the *loidoros* and does not give us permission to pressure the woman to avoid divorce.

PART IV

Paul Addresses
Six Marriage Situations

1 Corinthians 7

15 | Greek Believers Reveal a Misunderstanding

Before we discuss what Paul has to say about divorce, we will briefly review Jesus' comments about divorce. We saw that

- in Matthew 5, Jesus' words were intended to demonstrate our lost condition and our need for a Savior.

- in Matthew 19/Mark 10, Jesus' words were intended to censure the Pharisees and to strip from them the authority they had usurped, and then separately to explain to his disciples about remarriage.

- in Luke 16, Jesus briefly reiterates part of his Matthew 5:17-48 sermon.

In the passages where Jesus mentions divorce, we realized that he did not give a list of reasons when a man or woman could divorce and/or remarry after divorce, and from Jesus' confrontation with the Pharisees, we also realized that Moses did not have a list.

We will now investigate whether Paul has a list, and if he does, what might be on his list, but first we reiterate the importance of context.

It is often the case that the verses about divorce in 1 Corinthians 7 are taken out of their context and combined with verses found in a completely different context. For example, suppose a pastor is teaching on 1 Corinthians 7. As he comes to the verses that mention divorce in the passage, he might jump to Matthew 5:31-32, expound on "rules for divorce" that he thinks are there, and imply that this is the meaning in 1 Corinthians 7. When he does this without clarifying or differentiating the context of either 1 Corinthians 7 or Matthew 5:31-32, he commits both context mistakes. Again, be on your guard against these two mistakes.

Only two short passages in 1 Corinthians 7 are typically considered to refer to divorce. However, since we do not want to make context mistakes, we will work through all of 1 Corinthians 7 to ensure the divorce verses are kept in context.

1 Corinthians 7 Overview

Verse 1 is Paul's lead-in before he gives his advice and instructions. Paul begins,

Now for the matters you wrote about…

(1 Corinthians 7:1a, NIV[56])

Earlier in this letter to the Corinthians, Paul had been discussing various issues in the Corinthian church that had come to his attention from others. Now he changes his focus and will address specific issues the Corinthians themselves had sent him.

They had written,

It is good for a man not to have sexual relations with a woman.

(1 Corinthians 7:1b)

The Greek can mean either, "It is good for a man not to have sexual relations with a woman" or "it is good for a man not to have sexual relations with his wife."

This is the statement the Corinthians had sent to Paul. There is a wide range of thoughts and attitudes that could have generated this statement, such as:

- "Sex is not holy so I should be celibate."
- "Sex is defiling so I should be celibate."
- "Sex is 'okay,' but I can be holier or attain a deeper spirituality if I am celibate."

---

[56] Verses in Part IV are from the NIV.

- "Sex, even in marriage, is unholy or defiling so I should not have sex with my spouse."

- "Sex, even in marriage, is unholy or defiling, so I should divorce."

- "Sex with my unbelieving spouse is defiling so I should divorce."

Some Corinthians had reached the conclusion that they should be celibate for spiritual reasons. They had decided that sex was defiling or that abstinence was holier, including for those already married. They had the wrong idea, and in I Corinthians 7, Paul corrects them.

Because Corinth was a very immoral society and the believers' ideas about purity and sexuality were confused (to put it mildly), Paul presents six different marriage situations. In his teaching, he addresses whether sex is defiling or is unholy, he discusses how the Corinthians should react to the immorality they faced, and he teaches how they should consider the matter of sexual passion in regard to marriage. We will see that Paul's main purpose in 1 Corinthians 7 is to help the Corinthians think and respond correctly to the issue of sexual passion and sexual self-control.

The six marriage situations are:

1) vs 2-7   Advice to Believers Living in Immoral Cultures
2) vs 8-9   The Unmarried and Widowed Believers
3) vs 10-11 Divorce When Both Are Believers
4) vs 12-16 Believers Married to Unbelievers
5) vs 25-38 Virgins and Marriage
6) vs 39-40 Widows Only

As Paul discusses the six marriage situations in 1 Corinthians 7, we should recognize that he does not say everything we might want to know about marriage or singleness or divorce or widows or widowers. Nor does Paul discuss abusive marriages—he has already dealt with the abusive man in 1 Corinthians 5 and 6. The emphasis here is on sexual passion and sexual self-control.

16 | The First Marriage Situation: Living in Immoral Cultures

The immorality was so widespread in Corinth, some believers went to the extreme and concluded the only way to be truly holy would be to abstain from sex altogether. They had resolved, "It is good for a man not to touch a woman."

Paul himself thought it was good to be single, and he will give some reasons for his view later, but he did not believe this would be the best case for the majority of the Corinthians. He says,

But since sexual immorality is occurring, each man should have sexual relations with his own wife, and each woman with her own husband. (1 Corinthians 7:2)

Because the Corinthians were not able to withstand the sexual temptation from the immorality they faced, Paul advises them that sex within marriage is the solution. This was Paul's advice for them, but it is also good advice for all Christians everywhere who live in immoral cultures. And although Paul says this in the context of an immoral culture, the principles he sets forth apply to any person in any culture who thinks that the sexual relationship is not holy or is defiled.

But it is more than that they should marry. Paul adds,

The husband should fulfill his marital duty to his wife, and likewise the wife to her husband. The wife does not have authority over her own body but yields it to her husband. In the same way, the husband does not have authority over his own body but yields it to his wife. Do not deprive each other except perhaps by mutual consent and for a time, so that you may devote yourselves to prayer. Then come together again so that Satan will not tempt you because of your lack of self-control. (1 Corinthians 7:3-5)

Some Corinthians had thought that it was good for a man not to have sexual relations with his wife, but Paul contradicts them, "Not only is that the wrong way to think, each spouse actually *owes* the other spouse sexually."

One spouse is not independent of the other in the sexual relationship. The husband cannot consider himself a separate person from his wife and act as if his body is his own; likewise the wife. For Paul, each partner owing the other sexually is a proper attitude and is essential for married Christians who live in immoral cultures.

Paul mentions a reason to abstain from sex and that is to spend time in prayer, but even then, he states two conditions. First, there must be mutual consent. There is no place for being "so holy" as to choose to pray or participate in church or outreach activities instead of sex if both do not agree. Second, the period of abstinence should be limited—"for a time." Long periods of abstinence should be an atypical situation between husband and wife.

There could be other reasons a couple might agree to forgo sex (e.g., illness), but Paul mentions prayer, a spiritual activity, because some Corinthians had the idea that Christian activities combined with abstaining were holier or superior. That was a wrong assumption, and further, for those living in immoral cultures, this attitude could easily lead to trouble.

I say this as a concession, not as a command. I wish that all of you were as I am. But each of you has your own gift from God; one has this gift, another has that. (1 Corinthians 7:6-7)

Paul has a good understanding of the Christians in Corinth, and although he would rather more people were like him, that is, unmarried with sexual passion under control, he recognizes this is not the case for most of them. He considers that control is a gift. Again, in the context of verse 5, and in the context of this overall discussion that has to do with sexual passion, Paul's reason to be married has to do with the difficulty of controlling oneself sexually in an immoral culture. (Paul may think there are other legitimate reasons to be married, but that is not the issue at the moment.)

Paul's words are not a command—he will not go so far as to command people to marry.[57] Marriage is offered as a concession, but it is still good advice for most.

Summarizing verses 2-7, Paul's advice is,

- Being married provides people who live in an immoral culture an acceptable way to express their sexuality.
- Instead of not having sexual relations with one's spouse, and instead of being a spiritual celibate, husbands and wives owe each other to have sex.
- If you abstain from sex for a spiritual activity, you both must agree, and the abstinence should be for a limited time.
- Singleness, and the sexual self-control it demands, is a gift from God. If you do not have this gift, then get married and have sex.

We see then that sexual desire by itself is reason enough to marry—in fact, it is a good reason to marry. Marriage is for sex. Further, once married, it is right and helpful to proactively think of marriage in a sexual way.

In summary, when the Corinthians assumed it was good to be celibate, they were on the wrong track. If they, and we, cannot control our sexual desires and passion, marriage with a proactive sexual life is the solution.

A Practical Application

There are singles who would like to marry for the very reason Paul mentions but have not yet found a partner. Churches can help in this area by actively providing venues for like-minded singles to meet and get to know one another.

---

[57] In 1 Corinthians 7, Paul makes several statements such as "I say this as a concession, not as a command." We discuss these in Chapter 20.

17 | The Second Marriage Situation: Unmarried and Widowed Believers

Paul implies that many in Corinth do not have the gift of self-control that singleness demands. Therefore, to help the Corinthians withstand the immorality they faced, Paul advises them to see marriage as the God-designated plan for their sexual passion.

Does Paul include those who had been married before, but are now single? Should they also marry for this reason? He addresses those who are unmarried or are widowed believers in verses 8-9.

Now to the unmarried and the widows I say: It is good for them to stay unmarried, as I do. But if they cannot control themselves, they should marry, for it is better to marry than to burn with passion. (1 Corinthians 7:8-9)

Agamos

Paul mentions the "unmarried" four times in 1 Corinthians 7—in verses 8, 11, 32, and 34. Who are the "unmarried"? The Greek word for "unmarried" or "not married" is *agamoi* (the singular is *agamos*). We need to evaluate how the word is used in these four occasions in order to discover to whom it applies. We will go through each verse to see who *agamoi* refers to in that verse.

Verse 8, "And to the *agamoi* and widows, it is good for them to stay unmarried as I do…"

Here *agamoi* is plural and includes males and females. In this verse, *agamoi* is someone other than a woman who is a widow because widow is listed separately. These would include divorced men or divorced women or widowers (men) or possibly virgins (although since Paul specifically advises virgins in verses 25-38, he may not be referring to them here).

Verse 11, If she is divorced from her husband, "she must remain *agamos*…"

In this verse, *agamos* refers to a female.[58] *Agamos* is a divorced woman, clearly and unambiguously. Accordingly, the divorced, as a group, are definitely included in the ones Paul refers to when he says "the unmarried."

Verse 32, "The *agamos* is concerned about the Lord's affairs—how he can please the Lord."

Here *agamos* refers to a male. Since this verse is in the context of a larger section addressed to virgins, we should assume this man is a virgin. He has never been married; in other words, he is not a widower or divorced.

Verse 34, "The *agamos* and the virgin are concerned about the Lord's affairs…"

Here both terms, *agamos* and virgin, refer to females. In this verse, *agamos* refers to an unmarried woman, but not a virgin because virgin is listed separately. This *agamos* is a woman who has been married in the past and now would be either widowed or divorced.[59]

The above discussion of all four verses shows that *agamoi* includes:

- widows and widowers
- the divorced
- virgins

---

[58] In the Greek, we can tell whether *agamos* is referring to a male or female by the gender of the article used. For example, in verse 11, the article is feminine; in verse 32, the article is masculine.

[59] What if a man or woman was never married and also not a virgin? Paul does not address this specific situation, but he or she is unmarried and probably would be in the *agamos* group.

Verses 8-9

Now back to our passage,

*Now to the unmarried (*agamoi*) and the widows I say: It is good for them to stay unmarried, as I do. But if they cannot control themselves, they should marry, for it is better to marry than to burn with passion.*   (1 Corinthians 7:8-9)

This makes a total of nine verses that discuss sexual passion (verses 1-9). Again, sexual passion and celibacy is the main focus of Paul's words in 1 Corinthians 7.

In verses 8-9, along with the widows, Paul addresses the *agamoi,* which include the divorced and widowers (again, we can possibly include virgins, but since Paul later goes into great detail regarding the situation concerning virgins, it may be he does not include them here). So yes, those who have been married before, including the divorced, but are now single, should also marry for sexual reasons. Paul advises the *agamoi* and widows that if they have been married in the past and are now single, the same advice holds—it is better to marry than to burn with passion.

Notice Paul says it is *better* to marry than to burn with passion. This is similar to Jesus' words when he was asked by his disciples if it is *better* not to marry after divorce. We learned from Jesus it is *better* only for those who are eunuchs—those few for whom sexual passion is not an issue. Our gracious God emphasizes this conclusion by having Scripture address this from two sides, one expressed from the positive and one expressed from the negative:

- Paul tells us it is better to marry than to burn with passion—an affirmation from the positive
- Jesus' eunuch statement tells us it is not better to reject remarriage—an affirmation from the negative

Both Paul and Jesus tell us marriage after a divorce is fine—and for sexual reasons *it is better* to marry.

Paul said in verses 1-4 that it is good and helpful for people who live in immoral cultures to be married, and because of the immorality, to understand that he or she owes the spouse to have sex. Now, Paul specifically directs similar advice to those who have been married before. In this situation, Paul's advice to the *agamoi* is straightforward, "If sexual desire is an issue, then it is better to marry. Sexual passion is a good reason to marry."

There are verses in the New Testament instructing us to exercise self-control, and here in the matter of sex, Paul gives a practical step to help believers exercise self-control. That step is to be married and to have an active sex life. The reason why a person is single—whether divorced, widowed, or never married—does not change Paul's solution for those with sexual desire—marry and have an active sex life.

Paul states it quite unambiguously—for those who have been married before, *it is better* to marry again than to burn. Sexual attraction does not need to be denied. In fact, the situation is just the opposite—*it is better* to be married rather than to burn with passion. For most, in the matter of sex, it is better to marry than to insist on abstinence.

Since we know Paul uses *agamoi* to include the divorced, his statement contradicts those who say a divorced person cannot remarry, and of course, Paul's statement is consistent with Jesus' eunuch statement to his disciples (Matthew 19:11-12).

In spite of the consistency seen in statements by Jesus and Paul, some may possibly want additional confirmation from Paul corroborating that a divorced person can marry again. The next section provides additional confirmation.

18 | The Third Marriage Situation: Divorce When Both Are Believers

In the last chapter Paul said that it is better for the *agamoi* to marry than to burn, and verse 11 tells us *agamoi* includes the divorced. We now consider what further we can learn from verse 11.

There are two passages in I Corinthians 7 that use the word divorce. The first use is in verses 10-11 and contains the *only* verses in 1 Corinthians 7 that mention divorce between believers.[60] Just two verses,

> *To the married I give this command (not I, but the Lord): A wife must not separate from her husband. But if she does, she must remain unmarried or else be reconciled to her husband. And a husband must not divorce his wife.* (1 Corinthians 7:10-11)

These verses are often cited as proof that a Christian must remain unmarried if he or she has divorced.[61] We will evaluate them because there is more to these verses than first meets the eye.

Menetō

One of the reasons many of us believe a divorced person cannot remarry is Paul's command, "Let her remain unmarried." The word "remain" in the Greek is *menetō*. This word is used in the same tense, voice, mood, and person two other times in 1 Corinthians 7, verses 20 and 24.[62] Because context is always

---

[60] Paul does not specifically mention believers here, but in the next marriage situation, he refers to believers married to unbelievers letting us know he has switched topics from talking about believers married to believers.

[61] Some people think Paul is referring to legal separation in this verse. However, couples with a legal separation are still legally married. Since Paul says *remain unmarried*, we know he is referring to divorce, not legal separation.

[62] Present, middle, imperative, third person, singular, from *menō*. See Appendix D for more discussion about this word and 1 Corinthians 7: 20-24.

important to gain an accurate understanding of a passage, Paul's use of *menetō* in these two other places must be noted.

First, in verses 17-20, Paul says, "Remain uncircumcised." However, we know that for Paul, this does not mean "Never be circumcised" because Paul himself circumcised Timothy (Acts 16:1-3). Second, in verses 20-24, Paul tells slaves, "Remain a slave," but we know this does not mean "Never become free" because in Paul's next words, he tells slaves that if they are able to gain their freedom, they should do it.

Menetō is *conditional* in these two additional uses in 1 Corinthians 7. When Paul uses *menetō* in verse 11, we must realize that it has the same meaning as the two other times he uses it in this chapter—the use of *menetō* in verse 11 is also conditional and lets us know that "remain unmarried" does not mean "never remarry." Again, we see that context is invaluable for gaining an accurate understanding of divorce.

We will combine this insight of "remain" with Paul's other instructions to help us understand his intent in verses 10-11, but first, we will discuss some Greek grammar.

Passive, Not Active

The Greek verb for "separate," used two times in verses 10-11, is *chōrizō*. In this context, the word "separate" has the meaning "divorce," and we will use the word divorce in this discussion.

What is not obvious from most English translations is that both times the word is used, it is in the passive voice in the Greek. Yet, most versions translate the word in the active voice making it difficult for us to understand Paul's instructions.

Most translations, using the active voice, say:
v.10…a wife must not divorce
(aorist or present, **active**, imperative)

v.11… if she divorces
(present, **active**, indicative)

The Greek, using the passive voice, says:

v.10 …a wife not to be divorced from her husband…
(aorist, **passive**, infinitive)

v.11 …if she would be divorced…
(aorist, **passive**, subjunctive) [63]

Paul used an aorist passive infinitive in verse 10, which was an unusual choice that would have caught the attention of the Greek speakers in Corinth.[64] Although the passive was obvious to them, it is hidden from us when we read our English Bibles.

Using the passive as Paul did, verses 10 and 11 say,

(10) *And to the ones who have married, I command, not I but the Lord,* ***a wife not to be divorced from her husband…***

Stated more simply,

"I command ***a wife not to be divorced from her husband…"***

(11) *If she* ***would be divorced****, let her remain unmarried or be reconciled to her husband, and a husband is not to leave his wife.*

Indeed, if Paul had used an active voice in either verse 10 or 11, it would not have communicated the correction and instruction he intended. Paul used the passive voice because it best addressed the specific situation he wanted to correct (he was not addressing divorce in general). Next, we will combine our accurate translation of verses 10-11 with our understanding of *menetō* and with the

---

[63] In these two verses, we are chiefly discussing the change from passive to active voice, but it is also a concern that modern translations have changed the moods from an infinitive mood to imperative and from subjunctive to indicative.

[64] The following points help us see that *chōrizō*, used as an aorist passive infinitive in verse 10, is a unique grammatical construction:

1) In all of Paul's writing, he seldom uses aorist passive infinitives.

2) Although Paul uses *chōrizō* just seven times in his writings, this is the only place he uses *chōrizō* as an aorist passive infinitive.

3) In the entire Greek New Testament, when "I command" (*paraggellō*) is used, an infinitive usually follows, but the infinitive is never aorist passive, except in 1 Corinthians 7:10.

Corinthian situation (context) to discuss what Paul meant to convey in verses 10 and 11.

The Simplest Meaning

The simplest and most straightforward way to understand verses 10-11 is to keep the verses *in the context* of 1 Corinthians 7, which is within the context of sexual passion. More specifically, the context is about those believers who had concluded that sex was defiled or that abstinence was holier and that it would be better to be celibate.

Therefore, in verse 10, Paul is instructing those Christians who are still married not to be divorced (passive) because of this faulty theology—"Don't let this faulty thinking cause you to become divorced."

Further, it is likely that some Corinthians had already divorced because they thought sex was defiling or not holy. It is to these people Paul instructs that if the woman would already be divorced (passive) for this reason, she should remain unmarried. If the woman has not changed her mind about sex in marriage and still thinks it is defiling, then according to Paul's instruction, she should remain unmarried—and of course, it is obvious that someone who thinks sex is unholy or defiled should remain unmarried!

But the command to remain unmarried is not absolute; it is conditional. If she should change her mind about the sexual relationship (perhaps from reading Paul's letter, perhaps from conviction of the Holy Spirit, or perhaps from realizing that she would enjoy the sexual relationship after all), then she should be reconciled with her husband.

Keeping in mind the context of 1 Corinthians 7, what Paul is saying to husbands and wives is:

"To the ones who have married, I command (not I but the Lord) a wife is not to be divorced from her husband because she thinks that sex is defiled or that not having sex is holier. But if she would already be divorced for that reason, she must remain unmarried or be reconciled to her husband." (vs.10-11a)

Another way to say this is:

"Don't get divorced because you think that sex is defiled or that not having sex is holier. However, if you would already be divorced for this reason, then remain unmarried—unless you change your mind about sex. Then go get reconciled to your husband." (vs.10-11a)

This is the most likely and most straightforward meaning of these verses, and three things help us see it—the passive voice, *menetō*, and context.

The Corinthians Are Not Unique

The Corinthians thought being celibate would make them holier or keep them from being defiled, but they are not the only ones who have had these misguided thoughts. Throughout history, there have been people who believed that a way to achieve a higher level of holiness or a deeper spirituality was to be celibate.

In fact, most religions have at least one sect or religious order that believes this and practices it. It should not surprise us that Paul found it necessary to discuss and correct this thinking, and we can be thankful this wisdom is included in the Bible.

Pornography

Since we are talking about sexual passion, we should include a brief discussion of pornography and its destructive effects on marriage. Husbands often complain that the wife is not interested in sex, but at the same time, some of these same husbands wrongly suppose they can secretly view pornography and that it will not have an impact on the sexual relationship or the intimacy of marriage. This is completely erroneous thinking; pornography has a vast and destructive impact on the sexual relationship and the marriage.

Pornography destroys, even when the wife does not know her husband is sinning against her this way. How it destroys can be mysterious, but in such an intimate relationship, it is no surprise that the wife would sense there is something wrong. She might not be able to put her finger on it, but she knows there is a problem somewhere with the expected intimacy.

There is no inverse principle when it comes to pornography, as in "the less I look, the more my wife will be interested, so I can determine the amount of pornography I can look at based on how satisfied I am with my wife's interest." No. For the Christian man, there must be a complete rejection of pornography. And it is not hidden from God. There will be consequences. It is sowing destruction in your marriage and in your relationship with God.

Also, as pornography has become so much more easily available and ubiquitous, sadly more and more women are caught up in it. The same warning applies to females—it is not hidden from God, and it will sow destruction in your marriage and in your relationship with God.

Pornography is not an acceptable way for followers of Christ to express their sexuality. If this has been a problem in your life and you want to repent and be free of it, there is hope for you because we serve a great God. Start by telling the Lord your desire to obey him in this area and ask him to show you the next step to take.

19 | The Fourth Marriage Situation: Believers Married to Unbelievers

We now come to the second of two sections in 1 Corinthians 7 that mentions divorce. This is the marriage situation when one spouse is not a believer. The verses say,

> *To the rest I say this (I, not the Lord): If any brother has a wife who is not a believer and she is willing to live with him, he must not divorce her. And if a woman has a husband who is not a believer and he is willing to live with her, she must not divorce him. For the unbelieving husband has been sanctified through his wife, and the unbelieving wife has been sanctified through her believing husband. Otherwise your children would be unclean, but as it is, they are holy.* (1 Corinthians 7:12-14)

Some of the Corinthians had come to the erroneous conclusion that those who were married to unbelievers were clearly in an unholy or defiled situation. Therefore, in their misguided thinking, the believer should leave and end the marriage. It is quite plausible to assume the Corinthians had imagined this would be the best course for a believer so he or she could avoid this "defiled" relationship.

Paul's answer to their assumption is "no," and in fact, *his answer is just the opposite.* The unbelieving spouse and the children will be sanctified because of the believer. This is a wonderful thought for all Christians. We are not made unclean through our contacts with unbelievers (assuming we are not participating in their sinful activities). On the contrary, they are sanctified through contact with a Christian. The unbelieving spouse, either husband or wife, and the children of this marriage may very possibly be saved. This is, of course, a great motivation to stay married, and is completely the opposite of what the Corinthians had wrongly assumed. Paul is clear that this is not a reason to divorce.

The *chief teachings* we should glean from verses 12-14 are:

1. Sex with an unbelieving spouse is good. The unbelieving spouse is sanctified through the relationship with the believer. If the unbeliever is willing to live with the believing spouse, there is no problem.

2. This is not a reason for a believer to divorce. He or she can stay married and enjoy the sexual relationship.

Paul continues,

But if the unbeliever leaves, let it be so. The brother or sister is not bound in such circumstances; God has called us to live in peace. How do you know, wife, whether you will save your husband? Or, how do you know, husband, whether you will save your wife?

(1 Corinthians 7:15-16)

The Greek word translated as "leaves" in verse 15 above is *chōrizō*, the same word discussed in verses 10-11. Here, in context, the word means "divorce," so the phrase would read, "But if the unbeliever divorces."

In these two verses, Paul is talking about the situation when an unbelieving spouse divorces, or wants to divorce, the believing spouse. Paul just said in verse 14 that the unbeliever will be sanctified by being married to the believer. However, Paul does not want the Christian to think he or she should try to keep the marriage going if the unbeliever wants to leave in the hope that the spouse might be saved. Paul says, in effect, "What makes you think, wife, that you will be able to save your husband by staying with him? What makes you think, husband, that you will be able to save your wife by staying with her? If the unbelieving wife wants to divorce, let her go. If the unbelieving husband wants to divorce, let him go."

Paul says, "Let the unbeliever go; you are not bound to this marriage. Live in peace." The believing spouse can live in peace when he or she is willing to let the unbeliever divorce. The Christian must not create a conflict about the unbeliever's choice. The believing spouse can be at peace with the divorce because God's word says the believer is not bound to the marriage.

In this section of 1 Corinthians 7, "willing to live with her" and "willing to live with him" is *suneudokeō* in the Greek and literally means to agree with, to approve of, or to sympathize with (which we discussed in more detail in Chapter 13). Thus, this "willing to live with him or her" phrase refers to the case where an unbeliever who wants to stay with the believer understands the implications of being married to a believer and consents to them. The unbeliever understands that the believing spouse will live as a Christian and will express his or her life as a Christian and is accepting of this. There will be some unbelievers who would not be interested in continuing their marriage with a Christian, and Paul says, "Let the unbeliever go." The believer must not think he or she should to try to make the marriage last.

In the church today, we often hear that Paul means if an abusive husband wants to stay with his believing wife, she must let him stay. Paul means no such thing. First, we have already seen that Paul has dealt with the abusive man in 1 Corinthians 5 and 6—Paul calls the abusive man an unbeliever, instructs the church not to associate with him or eat with him, and commands the church to purge him from their midst. Second, the idea of *suneudokeō* does not describe the relationship an abusive husband has with his wife because an abusive man does not agree with, approve of, or sympathize with his wife.

Believers Married to Unbelievers—One More Point

Before we move on, it would be good to review one of Paul's further instructions to the Corinthians, which he wrote very shortly after his first letter. In 2 Corinthians, Paul is adamant that an unbeliever and a believer should not be unequally yoked,

Do not be yoked together with unbelievers. For what do righteousness and wickedness have in common? Or what fellowship can light have with darkness? What harmony is there between Christ and Belial? What does a believer have in common with an unbeliever? What agreement is there between the temple of God and idols? For we are the temple of the living God. As God has said:

"I will live with them
and walk among them,
and I will be their God,
and they will be my people."
Therefore,
"Come out from them
and be separate,
says the Lord.
Touch no unclean thing,
and I will receive you."
And,
"I will be a Father to you,
and you will be my sons and daughters,
says the Lord Almighty."   (2 Corinthians 6:14-18)

In any discussion involving marriage, we should keep in mind that Paul strongly maintains a believer and an unbeliever should not marry. In his first letter to the Corinthians, Paul was speaking to believers who had heard the good news, had become Christians, but were already married at the time they believed. Paul naturally addresses the situation where one of the spouses became a Christian and the other did not.

Since in 1 Corinthians 7:12-14, Paul spoke of marriages between believers and unbelievers, the Corinthians might possibly have assumed it was acceptable for a believer to enter into marriage with a nonbeliever. Paul clears up any misunderstanding about this in his second letter to the Corinthian church. Paul never condones a believer entering into marriage with a nonbeliever.

20 | The Fifth and Sixth Marriage Situations: Virgins and Widows

Virgins—The Fifth Situation

What about those who have never been married—what about the virgins? What is Paul's opinion concerning marriage for them? The fifth marriage situation is addressed in verses 25-38. Paul devotes more verses—fourteen—to this marriage situation than to any of the others.

Now about virgins: I have no command from the Lord, but I give a judgment as one who by the Lord's mercy is trustworthy. Because of the present crisis, I think that it is good for a man to remain as he is.　　　　　　　　　　(1 Corinthians 7:25-26)

The word translated "remain" in this verse is actually a verb of being (*eivai*, "to be"). Verse 26 more accurately says about virgins,

I think that it is good to be thus (a virgin).
　　　　　　　　　　　　　　　　　　(1 Corinthians 7:26b)

Paul again states his opinion that being single is good.

Although we cannot know for sure, the phrase "present crisis" could refer to a situation that put such constraints on people that they might find it especially difficult to meet the demands that come with marriage. Paul expresses the value of being single in trying times.

Then Paul gets specific,

Are you pledged to a woman? Do not seek to be released.
　　　　　　　　　　　　　　　　　　(1 Corinthians 7:27a)

The question "Are you pledged to a woman?" is most equivalent to "Are you engaged?" In Paul's day, when a couple became engaged, the engagement was almost as significant as marriage. (An example of this is in Matthew 1:18-20 where we see that during the time Mary and Joseph were betrothed, in verse 19, Joseph was called the husband, and in verse 20, Mary was called the wife.)

We can think of verse 27a as saying,

"Are you engaged? Do not seek to be released from your engagement."

Paul means, "I am not telling you to end your engagement." Breaking an engagement was serious, and in fact, a divorce was needed to end an engagement (again, the example of Joseph who had in mind to divorce Mary[65]).

Are you free from a commitment? Do not look for a wife. But if you do marry, you have not sinned; and if a virgin marries, she has not sinned.   (1 Corinthians 7:27b-28a)

By mentioning "free from a commitment," Paul is referring to a man whose engagement has ended. For these men, Paul advises they should not now seek a wife. Nevertheless, in spite of what Paul just said about being single, if they wish to marry, it is not a sin.

Next, Paul goes on to explain why those whose engagement has ended might not want to seek a wife and how those who are engaged should live as if they were not.

But those who marry will face many troubles in this life, and I want to spare you this. What I mean, brothers and sisters, is that the time is short. From now on those who have wives should live as if they do not; those who mourn, as if they did not; those who are happy, as if they were not; those who buy something, as if it were not theirs to keep; those who use the things of the world, as if not

---

[65] Matthew 1:19

engrossed in them. For this world in its present form is passing
away. I would like you to be free from concern.

(1 Corinthians 7:28b-32a)

We must keep these verses in the context of Paul's instructions
to virgins. Therefore, when Paul uses the word "wives" in this
section, he is still referring to those who are engaged, but not yet
married. Paul continues instructing virgins and says, "From now on,
those who are engaged to a wife should live as if you are not. What I
mean by this is, up until the day you wed, you have freedom from
the concerns and pressures that come with marriage—live like it!"

Paul elaborates on why those who have ended an engagement
might decide not to look for a wife,

An unmarried man is concerned about the Lord's affairs—how
he can please the Lord. But a married man is concerned about the
affairs of this world—how he can please his wife—and his interests
are divided. An unmarried woman or virgin is concerned about the
Lord's affairs: Her aim is to be devoted to the Lord in both body
and spirit. But a married woman is concerned about the affairs of
this world—how she can please her husband. I am saying this for
your own good, not to restrict you, but that you may live in a right
way in undivided devotion to the Lord.   (1 Corinthians 7:32b-35)

Paul makes a quick comparison between the unmarried and the
married and makes the argument that the unmarried are more
devoted to the Lord. In verses 25-26, Paul had said it is good to be
unmarried because of the present crisis, and now, in verses 32b-35,
Paul explains that a single person's interests are not divided, or at
least, a single person has the ability to have an undivided interest or
focus. Paul's chief point is that an unmarried person can be totally
devoted to the Lord.

However, secondarily, Paul includes something else of
importance about marriage in these verses. He says that the husband
is concerned about pleasing his wife and the wife is concerned about
pleasing her husband. For Paul, this is a natural attitude integral to
marriage. He does not suggest married couples change this attitude.

Nonetheless, we sometimes see in the church the belief that it is wrong to put the spouse in this special position. This may be suggested or taught for a variety of reasons and may even be done with good intentions, seeming to be more spiritual or a sacrifice for the kingdom of God.

This is not Paul's point, and it would not be normal or healthy for the marriage. And of course, some of the Corinthians had thought that it was good not to have sex with one's wife. They had thought abstinence was more spiritual. It is not; and in fact, it is normal for married people to have divided interests. (We have all observed many married couples very involved in working for the kingdom of God. However, Paul suggests that although it is not wrong to be married, these people could be more devoted if they were single).

If anyone is worried that he might not be acting honorably toward the virgin he is engaged to, and if his passions are too strong and he feels he ought to marry, he should do as he wants. He is not sinning. They should get married. (v.36)

But the man who has settled the matter in his own mind, who is under no compulsion but has control over his own will, and who has made up his mind not to marry the virgin—this man also does the right thing. (v.37)

So then, he who marries the virgin does right, but he who does not marry her does even better. (v.38)   (1 Corinthians 7)

In verses 25-35 Paul said it is good to be a virgin, and now in verse 36, Paul states a virgin may marry if he or she desires. The phrase "not be acting honorably" has the meaning in the Greek of acting in an indecent or shameful manner or improperly in a sexual way. Again, Paul gives sexual passion as a reason to marry.

The Greek for "if his passions are too strong" could also refer to a woman who is near her prime age for being married (this might be translated "if she is getting along in years").[66] "If his passions are too strong" seems the more fitting choice given the context. Paul says if a man is debating about marriage, and if he has strong passions, he should go ahead and marry.

In verse 36, Paul gives two reasons to marry—one, if the couple is acting improperly sexually, and two, if the man has strong passions (or they feel pressure from the woman's age).

In verse 37, Paul also gives two additional reasons not to marry—one, if the man, having control over his own will, feels no need to get married, i.e., he has his sexual passion under control, and two, if he has made up his mind not to marry.

It is fascinating that in the subject of marriage, one of the most important decisions a person can make, Paul says there is "Plan A," not to marry and wholeheartedly serve the Lord, and there is "Plan B," marry and have divided interests. Although the plans are quite different, and one will advance the kingdom of God more than the other, virgins (i.e., the never-been-married) are free to choose either plan, and both plans are acceptable.

There does not appear to be a "Plan C." In other words, Paul does not convey the option of combining with marriage that unique devotion to the Lord that often motivates an unmarried man or woman. For Paul, it seems to be one or the other. If a man or woman picks "devotion to the Lord in body and spirit," he or she should count the cost, and the cost is he or she should choose not to marry. Likewise, if a man or woman picks marriage, he or she should count the cost of marriage; he or she should expect to have divided interests and should give attention to pleasing the spouse.

---

[66] Daniel B. Wallace, *Greek Grammar Beyond the Basics: An Exegetical Syntax of the New Testament* (Grand Rapids: Zondervan Publishing House, 1996), 489
Max Zerwick S.J. and Mary Grosvenor *A Grammatical Analysis of the Greek New Testament*, Unabridged, 4th revised ed. (Roma: Editrice Pontificio Istituto Biblico, 1993), 512

The reasons Paul gives for why it is good not to marry could apply not only to virgins but to all unmarried people—widows, widowers, and the divorced. In fact, he mentions *agamos* in verse 34, "An unmarried woman (*agamos*) or a virgin is concerned about the Lord's affairs..." However, he specifically informs the virgins about these things because, having never been married, they would not have experienced these issues first-hand; they might think it is possible to live out a "Plan C." The divorced and widowed would have already experienced the pressures of marriage and most would have realized a "Plan C" is not feasible.

Finally, note that Paul does not say being single, being celibate, makes a person holier. No. What he teaches is that an unmarried man or woman has the opportunity and can give the time to more single-mindedly serve the Lord.

Widows—The Sixth Situation

In the last marriage situation, Paul will add one more reason for not marrying.

A woman is bound to her husband as long as he lives. But if her husband dies, she is free to marry anyone she wishes, but he must belong to the Lord. In my judgment, she is happier if she stays as she is—and I think that I too have the Spirit of God.

(1 Corinthians 7:39-40)

The last marriage situation is short. It is to women who are widows. Because Paul had just finished saying the unmarried can be more devoted to God's kingdom than the married, so that widows do not assume Paul is instructing them not to marry, he makes it clear with these two verses that the choice is up to the widow. The widow is free to marry anyone who is a believer, but Paul advises that, in his opinion, she will be happier if she stays single. Widows are able to live in full devotion to the Lord without the concerns and difficulties that come with marriage, but the choice is up to her.

21 | A Brief Review, Opinions vs. Commands, Christianity Is Unique, A Few Other Thoughts

In these six marriage situations, Paul gives advice and gives freedom to choose. Just two of the six marriage situations had to do with divorce—we will summarize those two.

Divorce Between Believers

In all these verses about marriage in I Corinthians 7, *only two verses* discuss divorce between believers, and in these two verses, Paul gives no guidelines or rules when divorce is allowed. What Paul says is that sex is not unholy or defiling so this is not a reason to abstain from sex in marriage or to divorce. Further, just as we discovered that Jesus had no list of rules when divorce is allowed and Moses had no list, we now know Paul had no list.

In addition, we learn remarriage after divorce is clearly allowed, and not grudgingly. In fact, Paul says it is *better* to marry than to burn with passion. This should remind us of Jesus' words to his disciples when they wondered if it is *better* not to marry after divorce. Jesus said it is better only for eunuchs.

Divorce Between Unbelievers

If a believer is married to an unbeliever, sex is to be considered sanctified, and therefore, is not a reason to divorce. If the unbeliever should want to divorce, the believer should let him or her go and can be at peace if this happens.

Also, we know from Paul's words in 2 Corinthians 6:14-18 that a believer should not marry an unbeliever. Paul's words in 1 Corinthians 7:12-16 are directed towards those who became Christians *after* they had married.

Opinions vs. Commands

Now that we have discussed the various marriage situations, we can make sense of Paul's "I say" statements. Paul makes seven of these "I say" type of statements throughout 1 Corinthians 7:

Verse 6   To those living in immoral cultures—"*I say* this as a concession, not as a command"

Verse 8a   To the unmarried and widows—"*I say*"

Verse 10a   To believers about divorce—"I command, *not I, but the Lord*"

Verse 12   To believers married to unbelievers—"*I say*, not the Lord"

Verse 25   To virgins—"I have no commandment from the Lord, but *I have* a judgment (an opinion)"

Verse 35   To virgins—"*I am saying* this for your own good"

Verse 40   To widows—"*In my* judgment (opinion), and I think I also have the Spirit of God"

Of the seven, 10a is the only verse that says "not I, but the Lord." What makes this situation different?

The context of verse 10 is a Christian divorcing another Christian because he or she thought that sex was defiled or that abstinence was holier. Paul states the Lord's command (not Paul's advice); it is a truth about marriage—it is not an opinion about marriage. Paul's command to the believing couple is, in effect, "Don't divorce because you think not having sex is holier." The implication is that these two believers should get their theology straight. Right thinking will eliminate this concern.

Consider also that Paul did not offer the opinion that the couple who had divorced for this reason should remarry. Although they had divorced based on wrong theology, he left them divorced (unless *they* changed their minds).

The other statements, which are Paul's opinions, are inspired by the Holy Spirit. They are opinions we can all hold, but they are opinions, not commands, because obviously…

Verse 6 - Paul will not command someone to marry. Hopefully none of us would either!

Verse 8a - Paul will not command someone to remain unmarried. Hopefully, none of us would either!

Verse 12 - Paul will not command a believer to stay in a marriage when the unbelieving spouse wanted out. Hopefully, none of us would either!

Verses 25 & 35 - Paul will neither command virgins to remain single nor command them to marry. Hopefully, none of us would either!

Paul is careful to say certain words are his opinion, and therefore, he allows freedom. We also should be careful to allow freedom.

Equality in Marriage—Christianity Is Unique

As we read through all of these instructions about marriage, notice how often husbands and wives are treated equally by Paul:

7:2   Each man should have his own wife.
Each woman her own husband.

7:3   Let the husband render his wife the affection due her.
Likewise the wife to her husband.

7:4   The wife does not have authority over her own body, but the husband does.
Likewise, the husband does not have authority over his own body but the wife does.

7:5   Do not deprive each other of sex except by consent (agreement).

7:8   I say to the unmarried (both men and women) and to the
        widows:
            It is good for them to stay unmarried, as I am.
            But if they cannot exercise control, let them marry,
            for it is better to marry than to burn with passion.

7:10-11   A wife must not be divorced from her husband
            (because she thinks sex is defiled or unholy).

        A husband must not divorce his wife
            (because he thinks sex is defiled or unholy).

7:12   If any brother has a wife who is not a believer and she
        is willing to live with him, do not divorce her.

        If a woman has a husband who is not a believer and he
        is willing to live with her, do not divorce him.

7:13   Paul uses *suneudokeō* to describe marriage, i.e., the
        husband and wife *together* agree that something is
        good.

Scripture describes much equality in marriage between the
husband and wife. This degree of equality is unheard of in many (if
not most) religions and cultures around the world. However, it is
found in those cultures influenced by Judeo-Christian thought. This
equality comes from the One True God and should leave us in awe
of this God.

Some Thoughts About the Apostle Paul

In the church today, the discussions and books that explain
when believers are permitted to divorce are seemingly endless.
However, notice Paul has not given reasons or rules for when a
divorce is permitted between believers. This is well worth noting
because, remember, Paul said about his life before he was saved, "I
conformed to the strictest sect of our religion, living as a Pharisee"
(Acts 26:5), and "I was advancing in Judaism beyond many of my
own age among my people and was extremely zealous for the
traditions of my fathers" (Galatians 1:14), and "I studied
under Gamaliel and was thoroughly trained in the law of our

ancestors. I was just as zealous for God as any of you are today." (Acts 22:3b). In the days before Paul's conversion as he lived as a strict Pharisee, he would have had no problem telling a man or a woman if and when and for what reason he or she was allowed to divorce. He would have had the rules, the exceptions to the rules, and the exceptions to the exceptions, well worked out—the fruit of generations of rabbinic teaching, all governing who could divorce and under what circumstances.

As typical of Pharisees, Paul previously would have applied the rules and exceptions and made his pronouncements. But here in our 1 Corinthians 7 discussion, as Paul is guided by the Holy Spirit and with the authority of an Apostle, we see he makes no authoritative pronouncements. This is in stark contrast to what he would have done before. Such an extreme change should catch our attention and be an example to us! Paul gave no reasons or rules when divorce is allowed between believers, and we ourselves must be careful not to fabricate such rules.

A Few Other Considerations

Many of us hold to rules and opinions about divorce that were not taught by Paul. For example, every book about divorce goes into great detail about one word, but Paul does not mention that word one time or even allude to it. What key word does Paul *not* mention? Paul does not mention adultery. He does not mention adultery once in 1 Corinthians 7. He does not tie adultery to divorce, and he does not tie adultery to remarriage after a divorce.

Notice too, if a couple decides to divorce, Paul gives no indication that anyone should look down on them or treat them as second-class citizens or expect them to repent.

Nor does Paul say (as we often hear), "You made a vow to your spouse; you must keep it" or "Marriage is a holy covenant that cannot be broken." Paul does not use these arguments (nor did Jesus). Similarly, in wedding ceremonies, we often hear the words, "Until death do us part." Paul does not teach this, but more importantly, the phrase is not found anywhere in Scripture. It does not come from our God—it is nothing more than a "tradition of men," (added to the Church of England's Book of Common Prayer during the 1500's and then finding its way into most Christian marriage vows). Those who add these words to the ceremony place on many a "burden hard to bear."[67]

Paul used only two verses to discuss divorce between believers, and the two verses are in a very limited context—divorcing under the false belief that abstinence was holier. We should not go beyond Paul's teaching when we talk about these verses.

---

[67] Possibly, at our wedding ceremonies, we should simply agree to marry—"Yes, I will marry you," and forego all the other vows and promises.

PART V

God's Attitude Toward Divorce

22 | Does God Hate Divorce?

What Does Malachi 2:16 Say?

At this point in our discussion, some Christians persuaded by this book's arguments may still wonder about Malachi 2:16, which is typically translated,

"I hate divorce," says the Lord, the God of Israel.

If our Lord did say this, it would be a verse that seems contrary to the conclusions presented so far, but does the verse actually say this? Recent scholarship has cast serious doubts on whether this passage says, "I hate divorce."

Let us examine the verse and its context.

Malachi 2:13-16 from the ESV,

13 *And this second thing you do. You cover the LORD's altar with tears, with weeping and groaning because he no longer regards the offering or accepts it with favor from your hand.*
14 *But you say, "Why does he not?" Because the LORD was witness between you and the wife of your youth, to whom you have been faithless, though she is your companion and your wife by covenant.*
15 *Did he not make them one, with a portion of the Spirit in their union? And what was the one God seeking? Godly offspring. So guard yourselves in your spirit, and let none of you be faithless to the wife of your youth.*
16 *"For the man who does not love his wife but divorces her," says the LORD, the God of Israel, "covers his garment with violence," says the LORD of hosts. So guard yourselves in your spirit, and do not be faithless.*

The English Standard Version translation presents an entirely different message than "I hate divorce, says the Lord." Did you notice the phrase is not there? Did you notice the word "hate" is not even included in verse 16 in the ESV? The closest it comes is a statement about a husband who does not love his wife.

Now consider verse 16, from the most recent edition of the NIV,

"The man who hates and divorces his wife," says the LORD, *the God of Israel, "does violence to the one he should protect," says the* LORD *Almighty. So guard yourself in your spirit, and do not break faith.*

In the NIV, the word "hate" does appear, but it refers to a human feeling, not God's. The emotion of hate is attributed to a husband.

The Septuagint confirms verse 16 does not say God hates divorce,

"But if you hate her and divorce her," says the Lord God of Israel. "Ungodliness will cover your thoughts," says the Lord Almighty. "Guard your spirit and do not abandon her." [68]

In the Septuagint, we also see the verse refers to a husband who hates and divorces his wife.

We can see in these three examples of verse 16 that there is no phrase where God says, "I hate divorce." There is no phrase where anyone says "I hate divorce." On the contrary, this verse refers to a husband who hates or does not love his wife and divorces her.

Instone-Brewer cites G.P. Hugenberger who translates the Hebrew as "if one hates and divorces."[69] Correctly understood, it is not God who hates, but the husband who hates.

---

[68] Authors' translation from the Septuagint. See also, www.ellopos.net/elpenor/greek-texts/septuagint/chapter.asp?book=42&page=2, accessed February 4, 2016.
[69] David Instone-Brewer, *Divorce and Remarriage in the Bible* (Grand Rapids: William B. Eerdmans Publishing Company, 2002), 54-58

We must accept that Scripture does not teach God hates divorce; this statement comes from an incorrect translation of verse 16. It may be difficult for the church to change its views about this verse after centuries of being taught otherwise. Nevertheless, the key concern is to guard against allowing our own ideas to shape Scripture (no matter how sincere our motives might be); instead, we want Scripture to shape our thinking and be our guide. Scripture does not teach God hates divorce.

What Does Malachi 2:13-16 Mean?

Each of these three versions translate the second phrase in verse 16 differently—

ESV – "covers his garment with violence"

NIV – "does violence to the one he should protect"

Septuagint – "ungodliness will cover your thoughts"

This phrase is considered difficult to translate, and we should be careful about what we read into it. However, verses 13-14 shed light on the issue God had with the Israelites—

Verses 13-14 from the ESV,

And this second thing you do. You cover the LORD's altar with tears, with weeping and groaning because he no longer regards the offering or accepts it with favor from your hand. But you say, "Why does he not?" Because the LORD was witness between you and the wife of your youth, to whom you have been faithless, though she is your companion and your wife by covenant.

Verses 13-14 from the new NIV,

Another thing you do: You flood the LORD's altar with tears. You weep and wail because he no longer looks with favor on your offerings or accepts them with pleasure from your hands. You ask,

"Why?" It is because the LORD *is the witness between you and the wife of your youth. You have been unfaithful to her, though she is your partner, the wife of your marriage covenant.*

Verses 13-14 from the Septuagint,

And these things which I hate, you were doing. You covered the altar of the Lord with tears and crying and groaning from your toil, yet he does not look on or accept the sacrifice from your hands as worthy. You ask, "For the sake of what?" It is because the Lord witnessed between you and the wife of your youth. You have forsaken her, your wife and partner of your covenant.

We see the following said of the husband:

ESV – you have been faithless to her

NIV – you have been unfaithful to her

Septuagint – you have forsaken her

Because these husbands had been faithless towards their wives, God no longer regarded their offerings. The wives are not ascribed any blame in this situation.

Summary

Malachi 2:13-16 should not at all be seen as a passage instructing that God hates divorce, but rather as God intervening to speak on behalf of wives whose husbands have been unfaithful, wives whose husbands have forsaken them through no fault of their own. These husbands were piously offering sacrifices to God as though nothing was wrong, but God tells these husbands that their offerings are no longer accepted because they had been faithless towards their wives.[70]

---

[70] This may have a parallel in I Peter 3:7, "Husbands, in the same way be considerate as you live with your wives, and treat them with respect as the weaker partner and as heirs with you of the gracious gift of life, so that nothing will hinder your prayers." (NIV)

This understanding is consistent with the other passages in Scripture that demonstrate God's concern for women and that he cares when they are dishonored by men in their lives. (See Appendix B for two other examples.)

Imagine how much more accurate our view of divorce would be today if Christians had not been taught through the centuries that God hates divorce!

23 | God Himself

When we hear sermons about Matthew 5:31-32, Matthew 19/Mark 10, Luke 16:14-18, 1 Corinthians 7, or Malachi 2:16, the focus often tends to be on how bad divorce is, and we are often left with the feeling that divorce is a sin. We suggest this idea is not biblically based, and we need to rethink this.

Looking back over the course of this study, we have learned that

1. Jesus' words about divorce in Matthew 5:31-32 were one of six "You have heard, but I say to you" statements used to drive home the point that we need Jesus to fulfill God's holy, righteous standard for us.

2. Jesus' mention of divorce in Matthew 19/Mark 10 was during confrontations with the Pharisees and during his follow-up discussion with the disciples. In these passages, he made three main points:

   a) Moses did not have a list of reasons when a man or woman is allowed to divorce,

   b) No mere human being has the authority to separate what God has joined; it is up to God alone, and

   c) Most divorced people are not "eunuchs" so we should expect they will remarry.

3. In Luke 16:14-18, Jesus very briefly reiterates his main point in his Matthew 5:17-48 sermon.

4. In 1 Corinthians 7

   a) just two verses discuss divorce between believers and they apply to a very specific situation—divorce under the false belief that sex was defiling, even in marriage, even between believers. Paul teaches that this is not a reason to divorce.

   b) Paul teaches that sex between a believer and an unbeliever is holy, and therefore, is not a reason to divorce.

5. Malachi 2:16 refers to the husband who hates and divorces his wife. It does not say, "I (God) hate divorce."

None of these previously mentioned verses state that a divorce is sinful (although some were opportune moments to do so). We must look elsewhere to understand how God views the act of divorce. There is one more biblical example of divorce to consider, and it will give us insight into whether divorce per se is sinful in God's eyes. What better way to come to an understanding than to look at God's own actions? Consider Jeremiah 3:8 where God says,

I gave faithless Israel her certificate of divorce and sent her away because of all her adulteries. (NIV)

God himself initiated a divorce.

If God, who does not sin, and "in him there is no darkness at all" (1 John 1:5), gave a certificate of divorce, then we must rethink whether there is something inherently wrong with the act of divorcing.

First, it should be clear from God's actions that divorce is not intrinsically wrong. God himself divorced Israel. We are forced to conclude that there is nothing inherently sinful about divorce.

Second, when God initiates or allows a divorce, it illustrates that our focus should be on the *cause* of the divorce—not the divorce itself. Israel's sinful *behavior* was the problem, and it was Israel's unfaithful behavior that led to the divorce. It was not God's certificate of divorce that was the problem.

Third, God demonstrates in Jeremiah 3:8 that some marriage behaviors are so bad the only answer is divorce. In fact, the divorce itself was a *right* response because what God does is always right.

We may feel inclined to rewrite Jeremiah 3:8; we may want to deny these words are true or make up other explanations of what the verse must mean, but again, we cannot change Scripture to suit our own standards, desires, or beliefs. It is likely that what needs to change is our view about divorce.

Consider—

- God gave Israel a certificate of divorce.
- God initiated the divorce.
- God sent Israel away.
- The divorce is not the problem; Israel's behavior was the problem.

When we talk about sin, *if we want to present the Scriptural point-of-view, we must not think of the divorce itself as sin. Instead, we must acknowledge the behavior that caused the divorce as sin* (we have God's perfect example to follow). We must be purposeful in doing this because it is easy (likely even a habit for many of us) to focus on the divorce instead of the sin that led to the divorce.

For example, if a woman leaves an abusive marriage, but the discussion focuses on how sad it is that there is another divorce in the church or that divorce is a sin or that "she got divorced!" or that she should have legally separated instead of divorcing, then we will have confused the issue by focusing on divorce instead of focusing on the sinful behavior that destroyed a marriage relationship. No, the discussion should instead focus on how sad it is that there is another abusive man hiding in the church, that abuse is a sin, and that we should expel the abusive man from the church.

It is the abuse, the infidelity, the irresponsibility, the lies, the selfishness, the pornography that will destroy a marriage; these types of behaviors separate a couple and can end a marriage. Divorce merely confirms that fact.

The devil would love for us to take our focus off the sin that destroyed a marriage and focus on the legal procedure instead, i.e., to focus on the divorce. Sadly, the devil has largely succeeded in taking our focus off the sinful and selfish causes. We will discuss this more in the next section.

Those who have divorced, and in particular, those who were wronged by their spouse, may have wondered if God understood what they were going through. Jeremiah 3:8 should be a comfort that God does understand. He understands the frustration and pain that comes from the sin that destroys a marriage. He understands the emotions that accompany the divorce decree, and He understands when divorce is appropriate.

Part VI

Practical Issues
and
Concluding Summaries

24 | Floodgates and Strengthening Our Marriages

Will We Open the Floodgates?

We all want marriages to last and be happy and healthy, and we would like divorce to be rare. Toward this end it is a good idea to provide thorough premarital counseling to prepare couples for situations that might arise. We should encourage couples to cultivate positive biblical habits and address sin in one's own life on a daily basis. It is also important to provide assistance for couples already married to help them work through tough times when they arise. These are good steps, and acceptable, but it is not acceptable for any of us to declare that a couple has or has not met some list of criteria for when divorce is allowed.

Some may be concerned that if we, the church, actually think of divorce in the biblical way presented in this book, we will open the floodgates for divorce. There are two answers to address this concern.

One, since we believe that Scripture is God breathed, and as such, is our authority, we need to guard against holding the traditions of men above the Word of God. We cannot rewrite Scripture simply to try to avoid an outcome we do not want, even if the rewriting seems more righteous. The Pharisees were good at adding their own additional rules to what God had already said, but in doing so, they only added heavy burdens onto people.[71] Eve also added additional meaning to God's command when she answered Satan in the garden, "God said, 'You shall not eat of the fruit of the tree that is in the midst of the garden, neither shall you touch it, lest you die.'" She wrongly added the words, "You must not touch it."

---

[71] "They tie up heavy burdens, hard to bear, and lay them on people's shoulders, but they themselves are not willing to move them with their finger." Matthew 23:4 (ESV)

Since the Word of God is our authority, we must align our teachings with the Word of God. We must be willing to teach what it says even if it makes us uncomfortable—and trust the results to God.

Two, the floodgates are already open. Divorce is already common in the church today; by some counts, we have almost as many divorces as the world. We are already flooded! It is time to re-evaluate our approach to divorce in the church. If our traditional approach is 1) not biblical, and 2) not working, why are we still doing it?

Some teach that good Christians must not consider divorce and must not even mention the word divorce. This may sound wise, but it is not a biblical teaching. Not only is this unbiblical, but it can also lead to much hypocrisy. For example, there are couples who obey this teaching, but all the while, their marriage is not functioning. The teaching that Christians must not divorce and must not even mention the word has not solved the problems in Christian marriages; this is a legalistic approach that ignores underlying problems. There are common-sense reasons why this has not helped, and instead, has likely *contributed* to the floodgates that are already open.

Of course, we should expect an unbiblical approach would not work out profitably in our lives. Furthermore, we should expect that dropping an unbiblical approach and adopting a biblical thought pattern will bring beneficial results. In this case, dropping the unbiblical teaching "never consider divorce" allows the biblical approach to lead us in a more practically helpful direction.

A Suggestion for Strengthening Our Marriages

Ignoring the possibility of divorce does nothing to rid the marriage of selfish behaviors that lead to divorce. We suggest that instead of forbidding the mention of the word "divorce," we should recognize that divorce can be a possibility. We should adjust our thinking to acknowledge that the *future* of our marriage relationship will be affected by *today's* behavior. If the husband or wife thought they had something on the line, i.e., something to lose (their marriage relationship), then they might treat their marriage more seriously.

In what other important area of our lives do we not acknowledge we have something at stake and act accordingly? Our job, raising our children, our money, our personal safety—we all understand that our choices affect the outcome of these—we might get fired, our children might make bad life choices, we might not have enough money to pay the bills, we might be injured in a car accident. We treat all these areas with fear and respect because we know our actions have consequences. Why do we not think of our marriages in the same rational way?

It is likely we do not think this way about our marriages because we are relying on a man-made "safety factor," which is "Good Christians never divorce." This "safety factor" is faulty, has been created from unbibilical thinking, and can be destructive. Not only does it not rid marriages of selfish behavior, we suggest it actually fosters selfish behavior—it *enables* us to be selfish.

Acknowledging that we have something on the line is simply recognizing there are consequences for wrong behavior, and recognizing consequences helps change our behaviors. Human beings respond to consequences—both positive and negative. Christians are no exception to this—we are all motivated by positive results. It is naïve to say we would live the same if there were no consequences, and we deceive ourselves if we think our marriages will be an exception. Saying Christians do not divorce is declaring, in effect, there will be no ultimate consequence for the sinful and selfish behavior that sometimes takes place in marriage.

By continuing with the faulty "safety factor," we are tampering with God's behaviors-have-consequences system. We are more than tampering—we are jettisoning one of the main protections for healthy marriages. When we cease to believe that bad behavior in marriage can have serious consequences, we remove a God-given, beneficial protection.

For example, if the husband thought he had something on the line, perhaps he would choose not to look at pornography. Instead, the thinking often is, "I'll quit when my wife finds out. There will likely be a bit of a fuss when she finds out, but because good Christians never divorce, she'll prove she's a good Christian wife by forgiving and forgetting, and we'll move on. Until then, I'll have my 'fun.'"

As a Christian, the wife should forgive, but that does not mean she must stay married to such a man. If he had understood that he had something on the line—the pain when his wife leaves him, the loss of respect from his children when they find out, the tearing apart of his family, and the shame when his friends, neighbors, and the church find out—maybe he would not have gone down this path of sin and selfishness in the first place. Instead, the "Christians don't divorce" rule *enables* him to continue in his sin.

Some behaviors such as adultery, pornography, alcohol abuse, lies and deceit, are obviously destructive and can lead to divorce by themselves. However, there are other, less obvious issues that cause trouble in a marriage such as money, education, free time, in-laws, discipline of children, the manner in which couples speak to each other, etc. The smaller behaviors by themselves would not normally lead to divorce, but when combined with other smaller behaviors, they often accumulate, become too much to bear, and lead to divorce. These smaller behavior areas must also be viewed as if there is something on the line.

We fool ourselves with the false, unbiblical thinking, "Because Christians do not divorce, my marriage is safe regardless of my selfish behavior." The divorce rate proves this is not true. We need to wake up!

Besides the fact that our method of not mentioning divorce and not allowing divorce is not biblical, *it is not working*. Too many marriages end in divorce now! We would be so much better off if we recognized that, in fact, our marriages *are* on the line. Once we recognize it and live accordingly, our marriages will be healthier and longer-lasting.

Biblically-based teaching will encourage us to evaluate our behavior to protect our marriages. Our response to, and the correction of, *our own selfish behavior* will be an effective guard against divorce. We should examine our own behavior for sin and selfishness—and repent and make changes. If we do not, we may find ourselves facing an end result of divorce.

Most couples want their marriage to last and be happy and healthy. Acknowledging the truth that we reap what we sow will encourage us to sow obedience now so that we will reap good fruit throughout our marriage.

Unintended Consequences—Food for Thought

Many people, when hearing about a woman in an abusive marriage, have wondered, "Why doesn't she get out? Why doesn't she leave?"

Now after our discussion, do you see her predicament? She is blamed if she does and is blamed if she does not. It may be that this woman is following the rule, "A good Christian must not consider divorce or even mention the word." This is perhaps the paramount (and most oppressive) reason why she does not leave her abuser. What a burden we, the church, have put on this woman! To the people who ask, "Why doesn't she leave him?" it may very well be that she is obeying this unbibilical rule we ourselves have taught her (because we mistakenly thought it was biblical).

If we want to help an abused woman, we should abandon our unbiblical view and send one message—that we support her efforts to leave this sad and dangerous situation.

25 | Concluding Summaries

In this book we have discussed so much more than divorce—the importance of context, how Jesus dealt with the Pharisees, how the Pharisees and the disciples differed in their reactions to various statements of Jesus, the nature of domestic abuse, that Paul addressed six marriage situations, and especially, Jesus' amazing salvation message in Matthew 5:17-48.

While these topics are all related, since this is a book about divorce, we will finish with a summary and a "30,000-foot" overview that focus on what this book has brought to light. The summary is more detailed while the overview provides a slightly different perspective.

Summary

This summary addresses the main points made in Parts I through VI of this book, and each part's summary finishes with very brief statements **in bold** of what each part said, or did not say, about divorce.

In Part I, we explained that we, the church, have typically made two context mistakes when it comes to Matthew 5:31-32, and we discussed the importance of 1) keeping the verses in their immediate context, and 2) not including them in a discussion with other verses that mention divorce when those verses are found in a different context. The nine questions in Chapter 2 helped make the point that, because we have typically been loose with the context, we have erred in that we often treat verses 31-32 quite differently than the rest of the passage (verses 17-30 and 33-48). In fact, there is no indication that Jesus' audience or the early church thought that Jesus "but I say to you" statements were meant to be applied literally.

After we pointed out that the Greek text in verse 32 contains the rarely used word *parektos* and examined its definition, we explained that Jesus used *parektos*, not to state his own position, but to acknowledge and then set aside *the Jews'* limited and narrow understanding about divorce. Jesus' emphasis was on the rest of his statement telling us that all marriage by or to a divorced person is adultery. There is no Exception Clause in Matthew 5:32.

With this insight, we realized that Jesus' purpose in verses 31-32, and in the whole Matthew 5:17-48 passage, is to demonstrate that it is impossible for us on our own, no matter how good we are or how hard we try, to satisfy God's holy standard of righteousness. This is the purpose of each of Jesus' six "You have heard, but I say to you" statements. God's holy, righteous standard is beyond anything we could ever attain or satisfy on our own, and we need Jesus to credit his righteousness to us. Matthew 5:17-48 is not a set of rules for Christian behavior. No! It is a wonderful salvation message!

There is no so-called Exception Clause in Matthew 5:31-32. In these two verses, Jesus was not teaching us rules for divorce, and he did not give us a list stating when a man or woman is allowed to divorce and/or remarry.

* * *

In Part II, we addressed Matthew 19:9 and learned that "except" is not the meaning of *mē epi*. There is no Exception Clause here either.

We also discussed three key statements Jesus made to the Pharisees about divorce. Jesus' first key statement occurred when the Pharisees asked, "Can a man divorce his wife for any reason at all?" In response, Jesus countered with the incisive question, "What did Moses command you?" The Pharisees had no answer because Moses never gave a list of reasons stating when a man could divorce his wife, and Jesus, with purpose and skill, pointed that out.

Jesus' second key statement occurred when the Pharisees asked him, "*Why* did Moses permit a certificate of divorce to be given?" They were again attempting to force Jesus to state a list.

Jesus did not state a list, but he did, in fact, declare why Moses commanded a certificate to be given, "Because of your hardness of heart he wrote you this commandment." The certificate is given to protect women from hard-hearted men like the Pharisees—Pharisees are the very type of people who make the protections of a divorce certificate necessary. It is important to keep in mind that Jesus did *not* say divorce was allowed because of hard hearts.

Jesus' third key statement (found nowhere else in Scripture) is his command, "What God has joined together, let not man separate." This statement means that no human has the authority to declare when or if a couple can divorce. It is up to God alone. This was a direct rebuke to the Pharisees because they had usurped the authority to say when a man or woman could divorce. However, it is also a command to us—none of us have been given the authority to say when a man or woman is allowed to divorce.

There is no Exception Clause in the Matthew 19 confrontation with the Pharisees. The so-called Exception Clause does not exist.

Jesus helped us discover that Moses did not give rules or a list stating when a man or woman can divorce and/or remarry, and again Jesus gave no list.

We also learned that when there is a divorce, a certificate is commanded to be given to protect women from hard-hearted men like the Pharisees.

Further, Jesus tells us that no human has authority to say when a couple is allowed to divorce.

* * *

Also in Part II, we discussed Jesus' explanation to his disciples when they were alone in a house. This private meeting would have been the most opportune time for Jesus to state his rules for divorce and/or remarriage, but once again, we see Jesus does not give a list.

The disciples had become alarmed at Jesus' statement to the Pharisees—could Jesus actually mean that if someone remarries after a divorce he or she literally commits adultery? Wisely, the disciples asked Jesus, "Then it's better not to marry!?" Jesus answers, in effect, "Only if you're a eunuch."

For most people, it is *not better* to reject or avoid remarriage after a divorce. It is not better, and Jesus himself tells us so!

And again we see that Jesus did not state a list of reasons when divorce is allowed.

* * *

We also saw in Part II that Jesus' fourth mention of divorce in Luke 16 is in the context of the law. The whole law must be fulfilled, and Jesus uses some of the same words and phrases in Luke 16:17-18 that he did in the Matthew 5 passage. Luke 16:16-18 is a very brief reiteration of Jesus' Matthew 5:17-48 message.

Once more, we see that Jesus did not provide a list of reasons when divorce or remarriage is allowed.

* * *

Part III examines Paul's words about abuse. A discussion about domestic abuse is included in this book because this is one of the main reasons why a woman might seek a divorce. The church has stumbled around in its thinking about this issue, chiefly because 1) we do not understand the nature of abuse, and 2) we do not recognize when the Bible does speak about abuse.

The church has typically discouraged a woman in an abusive situation from getting a divorce, and instead, has encouraged the husband to go to counseling or to anger management classes or to be set up with an accountability partner, all in order to salvage a marriage. Each of these approaches to the problem demonstrates a seriously inadequate understanding of the spiritual condition of the man, of the nature of abuse, and our instructions from Scripture.

Paul literally speaks about an abuser when he uses the word *loidoros*, which is defined as an abusive man (with somewhat more emphasis on the verbal aspect of abuse). Paul tells us that the *loidoros* must be kicked out of the church, that we are not to eat with him or associate with him, and further, he tells us that the *loidoros* is not saved.

Paul informs all of us how to view the abusive man, and he commands what actions we must take. In light of Paul's stern and sober words and commands to separate from an abusive person, divorce is clearly a biblical option.

* * *

Part IV discusses Paul's comments about divorce found in 1 Corinthians 7. The context of 1 Corinthians 7 is sexual passion and the conclusion by some Corinthians that it was good to be celibate. When we keep this context in mind, the verses referring to divorce are straightforward in their meaning.

Of the six marriage situations Paul discussed, only two had to do with divorce. They are 1) divorce between believers, and 2) divorce between a believer and an unbeliever. The immediate context of both situations is the same—some of the Corinthians had thought the sexual relationship was not holy or was defiled leading to the conclusion that they should not marry, and some had gone so far in this error that they had even divorced to avoid this "unholy" situation.

Paul corrects this error in thinking. In the situation of a believer married to *another believer*, Paul says that if one of them had divorced for this reason, then he or she should remain unmarried. However, "remain" is conditional, and the condition for Paul is that if the man or woman changes his or her mind about the sexual relationship, then he or she should reconcile with the former spouse.

Believers who were married to *unbelievers* had also felt that the relationship was defiled and should divorce. Paul corrects that reasoning and says the reality is, in fact, just the opposite—the unbeliever is sanctified by the believer. The believer should feel free to enjoy the marriage and the sexual relationship with the unbeliever. However, if the unbeliever wants to divorce, the believer should let him or her go.

Further, in this context, Paul states the principle, "It is *better* to marry than to burn with passion" (which reminds us of Jesus' eunuch statement to his disciples).

The sexual relationship is not unholy or defiled. Therefore, this is not a reason to abstain from sex in marriage and is not a reason to divorce (or for a single person to avoid marriage).

It is out of context to apply the words, "She should remain unmarried," to divorce as a general principle or to think that Paul meant *anyone* who is divorced must remain unmarried. The words are conditional and apply to specific people in a very specific situation—believers who had divorced (either from another believer or from an unbeliever) because they thought the sexual relationship was not holy or was defiled. Besides addressing this very specific circumstance and correcting their error in thinking, Paul has nothing else to say about divorce.

The divorced are part of the group Paul calls the "unmarried." When Paul allows or encourages the unmarried to marry, he reiterates the theme that it is biblically permissible for the divorced to remarry.

* * *

In Part V, we learned that Malachi 2:16 does not teach that God hates divorce, but in fact, God is rebuking the husband who hates his wife and divorces her, and God is explaining why this man's offerings are not acceptable.

We also realized that since it is true that God himself initiated a divorce, then there can be nothing inherently wrong with divorce, and in fact, it can be wholly right and a correct action to take.

The Bible does not say that God hates divorce. Since God initiated a divorce, we know there is nothing inherently sinful about divorce or wrong with it.

* * *

In Part VI, first we discussed that we should discard the rule that couples are not to mention the word divorce or consider divorce as an option; this idea is not found in Scripture. Further, it may be the very reason why some women never escape an abusive marriage. And second, we discussed the reality that divorce might be a consequence for the sinful and selfish behavior that sometimes takes place in marriage and acknowledged the Scripturally-based principle that there are consequences for our actions. In fact, wrong thinking in these two areas does not help marriage, but it actually *enables* selfishness and can be the cause of unhappy marriages, which, of course, exacerbate the conditions that might eventually lead to divorce.

We will see healthier marriages when we allow ourselves to admit that divorce could be a real consequence for sinful and selfish behavior and when we guard our behavior knowing there will be consequences.

The Bible neither bans the word divorce from conversation nor bans us from considering it as a possible consequence.

"30,000-Foot" Overview

The following is a list of key points **we learned in this book, the essence of what the New Testament tells us about divorce**:

- It is *not better* to reject or avoid remarriage after a divorce. It is not better and Jesus himself tells us so!

- Only for "eunuchs," those with no sexual desire, is it better to not marry after divorce, which means there are *very few* people to whom not marrying will apply.

- Divorce was and is allowed; the *command* was to give a certificate of divorce.

- A certificate of divorce was commanded to be given as a protection for women, especially from hard-hearted men like the Pharisees.

- No human being has the authority to say when a couple may or may not divorce—this is up to God alone.

- Sex in marriage is not unholy or defiling even if married to an unbeliever, and therefore, is not a reason to divorce.

- "Remain unmarried" is conditional and context tells us it applies only to those who had already divorced because they thought sex was unholy or defiled.

- If anyone had divorced due to the erroneous belief that sex in marriage was unholy but then changed his or her mind, he or she should reconcile with the former spouse.

- It is *better* to remarry than to burn with passion.

- There is nothing inherently wrong or sinful with divorce.

- Paul does not tell women to stay in an abusive marriage. (Given Paul's stern and sober commands about abusive men, this is no surprise.)

We have learned many things in this book, but we also see that **we must "unlearn" or let go of the following unbiblical ideas**:

- That there is a so-called Exception Clause in the Bible (there is not).

- That there is a list of rules when divorce is allowed (there is no list).

- That Jesus wanted us to literally apply his "You have heard, but I say to you" statements (he had a different purpose for these words).

- That a pastor or church leader, or anyone else, has the right to say a person may divorce or not (no human has this right).

- That "Remain unmarried" is a general principle for anyone who is divorced (it is an instruction only for those in a very specific situation).

- That the Bible says God hates divorce (it does not).

Final Thoughts

1. None of us has the right to tell a man or woman if or when he or she can divorce and/or remarry—no human is given this authority.

2. We have been given no list of rules when divorce and/or remarriage is allowed. Moses had no list. Paul had no list. Jesus had no list. To be biblical in our thinking, *we ourselves* must jettison any list that we might have.

3. When it comes to questions of divorce, a Christian man or woman in a troubled marriage should seek God's will in the matter, just as they would seek God's will in any matter.

These three conclusions might cause some of us to be concerned that there will now be more divorces in the church. That is a possibility. However, on the other hand, it might be the case that we will see *fewer* divorces because we will *stop* giving the green light for divorce based on a non-existent Exception Clause. How many couples have been given the go ahead to divorce based on a mistaken belief in a non-existent Exception Clause?

We have no idea which couples God would give permission to divorce or which couples God would want to stay together and work through the issues, and therefore, we should encourage couples to seek God's will in the matter.

It is very possible that if we 1) jettison our belief about an Exception Clause, 2) jettison our lists, and 3) allow potential consequences to correct our selfish and sinful behavior, we will have *fewer* divorces in the church.

APPENDICES

Appendix A | *Parektos* in Two Other Verses

As discussed in Chapter 3, in Matthew 5:32, Matthew did not use the Greek words that are usually translated "except." Instead, he used the work *parektos*. (See Chapter 3 for the discussion about the definition of *parektos*.)

Parektos is used just three places in the Greek New Testament (and not at all in the Septuagint). In Chapter 3, we discussed its use in Matthew 5:32. In this appendix, we will briefly look at the other two places where *parektos* is used in the New Testament.

Acts 26:27-32

In Acts 26:27-32, both *parektos* and *ei mē* are used, and we can easily see the difference,

Paul said, "You believe, King Agrippa, in the prophets? I know that you believe." v. 27
And Agrippa said to Paul, "In such little time you are persuading me to make me a Christian?" v. 28
*And Paul said, "I pray to God even in a little or a lot of time, not only you, but also all the ones hearing me today will become even like I am, besides (*parektos*) these bonds."* v. 29
And the King and the Governor and Bernice and the ones who were sitting with them left the room and were speaking with one another saying, "This man has done nothing worthy of death or bonds." v. 30-31
*And Agrippa said to Festus, "This man was able to have been released except (*ei mē*) he has appealed to Caesar."* v. 32

In the *parektos* sentence, the focus is on Paul's hope and prayer that the ones hearing him will become Christians; his bonds are not the point and are de-emphasized or diminished in consideration. This is why parektos should be translated with the idea of "besides." It would be helpful if the *parektos* clause was placed in parentheses,

And Paul said, "I pray to God even in a little or a lot of time, not only you, but also all the ones hearing me today will become even like I am (besides these bonds)." v. 29

In the *ei mē* sentence, the focus is on the fact that Paul had appealed to Caesar. *Ei mē* emphasizes that it was Paul's appeal to Caesar that kept him from being released.

2 Corinthians 11:28

The third New Testament verse that uses *parektos* is when Paul lists the trials and dangers he has faced as a Christian and as an Apostle. He says,

"Besides (parektos) *everything else, I face daily the pressure of my concern for all the churches. "*   (2 Corinthians 11:28)

In this sentence the focus is the daily pressure on Paul that comes from his concern for all the churches. "Except" would not be a reasonable translation. Again, it would be helpful if the *parektos* clause was placed in parentheses,

"(Besides everything else), I face daily the pressure of my concern for all the churches."

Conclusion

We can see that in these other two places where *parektos* is used, the meaning "besides" or "apart from" or "outside of" is confirmed.

Appendix B | Divorce and Remarriage at the Time of Jesus

We as Christians may have varying ideas of what marriage and divorce looked like in the first century. We might tend to think the Jews very rarely divorced. For our study about divorce, it is important and helpful to recognize the fact that divorce and remarriage was practiced and accepted in Old Testament times and also at the time Jesus was teaching. Without this understanding, we might make the wrong assumptions about the state of marriage, divorce, and remarriage in the first century, and we might miss what Jesus wanted us to hear. We do not know for sure what percentage of first century Jews divorced, but there are several reasons to believe divorce was not uncommon, and in fact, divorce was an accepted fact of life in NT times.[72]

David Instone-Brewer relates that in the first century BC, divorce was common enough among the Jews that officials tried to regulate the bride price and/or the dowry in an attempt to limit divorce.[73] Society had found that, in general, if the dowry was high, the marriage rates slowed but the divorce rates rose (the dowry was paid by the father of the bride and would be claimed by the bride for her use if she was divorced or was widowed); if the dowry was lower, it was easier to marry but less monetarily lucrative for the wife to divorce.

Instone-Brewer also says that during the last two centuries BC and the first century AD, divorce had become easier for women to initiate—for both Jewish and Greco-Roman women.[74]

---

[72] Colin Brown general ed., *The New International Dictionary of New Testament Theology*, Vol. 1, (Grand Rapids: Zondervan Publishing House, 1971), 506
[73] David Instone-Brewer, *Divorce and Remarriage in the Bible* (Grand Rapids: William B. Eerdmans Publishing Company, 2002), 19, 81-84
[74] Ibid. p. 72

Old Testament Passages About Divorce

To have some idea of first-century Jewish thinking about divorce, we should, of course, consider the Old Testament. We might be surprised at how little the Old Testament mentions divorce, and we might be especially surprised that the verses speak of divorce in a matter-of-fact way, not negatively.

Only Two Old Testament Passages Prohibited *Divorce*

There are only two Old Testament passages that prohibited divorce, and they apply only to two very specific circumstances.

Deuteronomy 22:13-19 says if a man accused his wife of not being a virgin when he married her, and after it was proven she had been a virgin, he would never be able to divorce her because he defamed her.

Deuteronomy 22:28-29 says if a man seduced (or possibly, raped) a woman, he would have to marry her and never divorce her.[75]

These are the only two references that say when someone *could not* divorce, and both are given as a measure of protection for women. The prohibitions apply to men only. Further, Moses' two reasons when a man could not divorce have more to do with justice than they have to do with a principle about divorce. In addition, the

---

[75] This passage is often mocked by non-believers because they think this gave men license to seduce or rape; instead, this rule required the man to be accountable to a family and give up future plans he might have had for himself. More importantly, this rule provided protection for the woman—in most cultures at that time (and still in some cultures today), this woman might have been unable to find a husband who would marry her after this happened. This rule protected her from never being able to marry, a situation that could be very difficult for a woman in some cultures. And worse, in some cultures of that day (and still in some cultures today) the woman would have been the one who was punished, for example, by stoning or lashing. In contrast, the Jewish woman's future was protected; she had an option of marriage, but she was not forced to marry this man. She could marry any other man or she could not marry at all. And although the seducer could not divorce her, the woman could divorce him. Instone-Brewer says "Amram points out that Philo and Josephus both assumed that in Judaism the choice lay with the woman." David Instone-Brewer, *Divorce and Remarriage in the Bible* (Grand Rapids: William B. Eerdmans Publishing Company, 2002), 28

need for two specific passages to say when divorce was prohibited implies that divorcing in general was permitted.

Two Old Testament Circumstances Prohibited *Remarriage* after Divorce

There are only two circumstances in the Old Testament in which remarriage after divorce was prohibited, and they are very specific.

The first is mentioned in Deuteronomy 24:1-4/Jeremiah 3:1. These verses say a man could not remarry a woman he had previously divorced if she had married and divorced someone else after the first divorce—the first husband was not allowed to marry her again.

The second is in Leviticus 21:7,14/Ezekiel 44:22. A priest could not marry a divorced woman (or a widow or a prostitute). This restriction applies only to males.

These are the only two reasons given for when remarriage is prohibited, and they are quite specific.

The Same Two Old Testament Circumstances Show Marriage after Divorce Was *Permitted*

By stating who could not remarry after a divorce, these same passages (Deuteronomy 24:1-4/Jeremiah 3:1) imply that a man was allowed to remarry after divorce in any other circumstance. And, by prohibiting one specific third-marriage situation, the verses imply a man or woman could marry a second and even a third time after divorce. The verses state only that after divorcing wife number two, a man could not remarry wife number one.

Similarly, in Leviticus 21:7,14/Ezekiel 44:22, while forbidding priests to marry a divorced woman (or widow or prostitute), the verses imply others could and would marry a divorced woman (or widow or prostitute).

Other Old Testament Verses that Mention Divorce

Along with Malachi 2:16 and Jeremiah 3:8, which are discussed in Part V of this book, a few other verses mention divorce. Though the following do not provide much more information about divorce, they are the bulk of the remainder of Old Testament verses about divorce:

Leviticus 22:13: If a priest's daughter became a widow or was divorced and had no children, she was allowed to return to her father's house and eat the priest's food. Divorce is not treated negatively here; in fact, she can eat the *priest's* food.

Numbers 30:9: The vow of a widow or a divorced woman stood. Divorce is simply a fact and does not inhibit a woman's ability to make socially and religiously binding commitments.

I Chronicles 8:8: A man named Shaharaim sent his wives away (he may or may not have divorced them).

Ezra 10:11, 19: Those Jews who had married foreign women were commanded to separate from them and put them away.

In churches today, the protection of a marriage is often held up as the highest priority, but in the Ezra verses, we see protecting the marriage was not the ultimate concern. The ultimate concern was being faithful to God, and in fact, the divorces were commanded and seen as a positive step. The verses in Ezra give us an example that keeping a marriage together is not always the highest good and shows us that divorce was a Biblical option.

To summarize, although Moses did not give a list of reasons why someone could divorce, he gave two reasons, and only two, why someone *could not* divorce. These two reasons are very specific, and they restrict only men—not women. Also, we should likely consider that these two verses address justice and protection for women more than they address divorce per se.

Other Times Where We See Divorce and Remarriage Was an Accepted Practice

Under Mosaic Law, the wife was given a certificate of divorce by her husband. This certificate essentially verified her divorce and stipulated she could freely remarry—the Jewish standard form of divorce certificate explicitly allowed the right to remarry. In fact, remarriage was normal and even expected after divorce.[76]

Instone-Brewer states that as far as marriage was concerned, there were many similarities between ancient Israel and nearby cultures, but the Jewish divorce certificate *was unique to the ancient Jewish culture.*[77] As discussed in Chapter 6, the divorce certificate protected the woman from a husband who might say, "I divorce you," but would later go back on his word. Without a certificate, the woman would not be able to verify that she was truly divorced. The certificate verified she was divorced, and it verified she was free to marry again. To be divorced was to be able to marry again.

The Pharisees' actions and stances about divorce show the practice was not uncommon. They had two schools of thought about divorce—the Shammais and the Hillels. Each group of Pharisees had their own set of rules. This indicates that divorce was common enough that rules were discussed, articulated, and delineated. It also shows divorce was accepted if the rules were followed.[78]

Along with this, the Hillel group of the Pharisees was known for allowing divorce for almost any reason, which shows it was possible to obtain a divorce easily and implies divorce may have been relatively frequent.

---

[76] David Instone-Brewer, *Divorce and Remarriage in the Bible* (Grand Rapids: William B. Eerdmans Publishing Company, 2002), 117

[77] Ibid., pp. 32-33

[78] For a list of some of the differences between Hillel and Shammai divorce rules, see Barbara Roberts, *Not Under Bondage: Biblical Divorce for Abuse, Adultery & Desertion* (Maschil Press 2008), 134

In *Sketches of Jewish Social Life in the Days of Christ*, Alfred Edersheim says even the stricter Pharisees (Shammais), allowed divorce for a wide variety of reasons. Some of their grounds for a man to divorce his wife included "going about with loose hair...familiarly talking with men, ill-treating her husband's parents in his presence, brawling, that is, 'speaking to her own husband so loudly that her neighbors could hear her in the adjoining house,' gossiping in the streets, and immodest behavior in public."[79] A wife could insist on a divorce if her husband "were a leper, or affected with polypus, or engaged in a disagreeable or dirty trade, such as that of a tanner or a coppersmith."[80]

The point is that divorce was an accepted practice at the time Jesus taught Matthew 5:31-32. The Jewish community did not place the same heavy stigma on divorce, or remarriage after divorce, that the church has put on it.

Women's Rights in Marriage

We sometimes wonder if a woman was permitted to divorce a husband. Although mentioned already, it is good to reiterate. We can see from Edersheim's examples in the previous section that they were able to. Also, if a father had betrothed his young daughter to a future husband, Edersheim says that she had the right to insist on a divorce when she reached the age of 12 years and two days.[81]

Jesus confirms a woman could divorce her husband, "Anyone who divorces his wife and marries another woman commits adultery against her. *And if a woman divorces her husband* and marries another man, she commits adultery" (Mark 10:11-12).[82]

---

[79] Alfred Edersheim, *Sketches of Jewish Social Life in the Days of Christ* (New York: James Pott & Co., 1881), 157
[80] Ibid., p.158
[81] Ibid., p.144 (Divorce was needed to end a betrothal.)
[82] The point of mentioning this verse here is to show that a woman could divorce a husband.

We might also wonder if a woman was allowed to refuse to marry someone. Edersheim says, "But, at any rate, the woman had, in case of betrothal or marriage, to give her own free and expressed consent, without which a union was invalid."[83]

We see this freedom demonstrated in Genesis 24 when Abraham sends his servant to find a bride for his son Isaac. When the servant found that Rebekah was the answer to his prayers, and after a consultation with her mother's family and brother, we read her mother and brother said, "We will call the girl and consult her wishes." They asked Rebekah, "'Will you go with this man?' And she said, 'I will go'" (verses 57, 58).

---

[83] Alfred Edersheim, *Sketches of Jewish Social Life in the Days of Christ* (New York: James Pott & Co., 1881), 143

Appendix C | Background Information on the Pharisees

The historian Josephus wrote that although there were Pharisees as far back as 161-143 BC, the Pharisees as a party were at their greatest prominence and authority when Jesus arrived on the scene.[84] They were one of the parties that made up the Sanhedrin, the highest Jewish court, which held civil authority and some criminal authority.[85]

Although the Jews were under Roman rule at the time of Jesus, they were allowed to adhere to their own laws and traditions, and the Pharisees held legal jurisdiction with Roman approval. The Pharisees were considered experts on Jewish law, and the people held the Pharisees in respect and also some fear.

John 9 is a good example to demonstrate that the people regarded the Pharisees as authorities. Jesus had healed a man blind from birth. In verse 13 we read, "They brought to the Pharisees the man who had formerly been blind."

Why did the people bring him to the Pharisees? They brought him because they were accustomed to the Pharisees making pronouncements; the people considered it standard procedure for the Pharisees to give statements of approval or disapproval for behavior and events.[86]

---

[84] http://www.newworldencyclopedia.org/entry/Pharisees, accessed February 4, 2016.
Barbara A Chernow and George A Vallaski, ed., *The Columbia Encyclopedia*, 6th ed. (Houghton Mifflin, 2015), accessed online,
http://www.encyclopedia.com/topic/Pharisees.aspx
[85] Acts 23:6 tells us the Sanhedrin at that time was made up of Sadducees and Pharisees.
[86] This is a different scenario than Matthew 8:1-4, where Jesus told the man healed of leprosy to go show himself to the priest. The priests *had* been given authority by God to declare leprous people clean in order for them to be welcomed back into society (Leviticus 14).

However, this power to make pronouncements was inherently intimidating because the Pharisees also had the power to put people out of the synagogue. We see in John 9:18-22 that the Pharisees summoned the parents of the man born blind and questioned them. The parents said, "We know that this is our son, and that he was born blind. But by what means he now sees, we don't know or who opened his eyes, we don't know. He is of age, ask him. He will speak for himself." Scripture tells us the reason the parents said this—*they were afraid* (v.22). They were afraid because it had been previously decided that if anyone would confess that Jesus was Christ, that person would be put out of the synagogue.

In fact, "put out of the synagogue" is not a verb in the Greek. It is an adjective meaning a put-out-of-the-synagogue person. It is more of a stigma than an action; it is deeper than a one-time event, a stigma the Jewish people would want to avoid at all costs. As the place of public worship, the synagogue was the heart of each community and the chief means of uniting Jews scattered throughout the world.

If a man or woman became a put-out-of-the-synagogue person, he or she would be isolated from nearly all sources of community because the man or woman would be excluded from many Jewish social or business activities. Further, as a Jew, associations and dealings with Gentiles would also be limited.

In addition to putting people out of the synagogue, the Pharisees exercised the power to arrest people, which was tied to the power they had from the Sanhedrin. We read in John 11:57, "The chief priests and Pharisees had given orders that if anyone found out where Jesus was, he should report it so that they might arrest him."

Also, the Apostle Paul, not yet saved and acting with the authority of a Pharisee, "was destroying the church and going into house after house, dragging out both men and women, delivering them to prison" (Acts 8:3).

There are over forty Gospel passages that mention the Pharisees. A quick overview of some pertinent passages will show their hostility to Jesus:

The Pharisees--

- Sent their attendants in an (unsuccessful) attempt to arrest Jesus. (John 7:32)

- Called Jesus a Samaritan and demon-possessed. (John 8:48)

- Asked for a sign from heaven to test Jesus. (Matthew 16:1-4)

- Picked up stones to stone Jesus. (John 8:59)

- Plotted to kill Jesus. (Mark 3:1-6)

- Said Jesus drives out demons by Beelzebub. (Matthew 12:24)

- Looked for a reason to accuse Jesus. (Luke 6:6-11)

- Opposed him and besieged him with questions, lying in wait to catch him in something he might say. (Luke 11:53-54)

- Ordered that if anyone found out where Jesus was, he should report it so they might arrest him. (John 11:57)

- Along with the chief priests, sent their soldiers and officials—with Judas—to arrest Jesus. (John18:3)

In Part II, we discussed two times the Pharisees confronted Jesus, but Jesus also confronted the Pharisees. Matthew chapter 23 gives many examples of Jesus' strong statements made to the Pharisees. For example, verse 15 says, "Woe to you, teachers of the law and Pharisees, you hypocrites! You travel over land and sea to win a single convert, and when he becomes one, you make him twice as much a son of hell as you are."

Parenthetically, although the majority of Pharisees are seen as antagonistic to him and opposed to following him, any of the Pharisees at any time could have decided to seek and follow Jesus. For example, Nicodemus was a Pharisee who did seek out Jesus and asked good questions as we see in John 3. He asked as one who was interested in following and as one who wanted to know how to apply Jesus' teachings to his own life. Later, he helped with Jesus' burial (John 9:38-42). Acts 15:5 gives the example of a group of Pharisees who became believers, and of course, the Apostle Paul at one time had been a Pharisee (Acts 26:5).

Two Practical Applications

Divorce is not the only area where Jesus' statements to the Pharisees were different than his statements to the crowds. It is a fascinating, worthwhile study to look into this more as you read the gospels. Ask yourself two questions when reading Jesus' words: Who is he talking to, and is this different than when he speaks on the same topic to others?

A second practical application is that there will always be people in our congregations who desire power similar to the Pharisees, and there will always be people who will give up their freedom to them. This is a reminder to be on guard that we do not give up our freedom to those who have usurped power and be on guard that we ourselves do not wield such power over others.

Appendix D | Paul's Use of the Word "Remain"

Menetō

Because the idea that a divorced person must remain (*menetō*) unmarried for life has been ingrained in our thinking, we will take time to consider "remain" more closely in its context. To get a better understanding of this, we will examine Paul's use of *menetō* in the two other places it is used in 1 Corinthians 7 because, again, context must be taken into account.

Besides 1 Corinthians 7:11, Paul uses this same word, *menetō*, in the same tense (present), the same person (third singular), and the same mood (imperative), in two additional verses in 1 Corinthians 7, verses 20 and 24.

The first is found in verses 17-20,

*Nevertheless, each person should live as a believer in whatever situation the Lord has assigned to them, just as God has called them. This is the rule I lay down in all the churches. Was a man already circumcised when he was called? He should not become uncircumcised. Was a man uncircumcised when he was called? He should not be circumcised. Circumcision is nothing and uncircumcision is nothing. Keeping God's commands is what counts. Each person should remain (*menetō*) in the situation they were in when God called them.* (1 Corinthians 7:17-20)

When Paul uses *menetō* in the context of circumcision, does he mean never be circumcised? Or are there reasons a male might be circumcised? Are there exceptions to *menetō*?

Paul himself gives us the answer by making an exception to his own teaching,

Paul came also to Derbe and Lystra. A disciple was there, named Timothy, the son of a Jewish woman who was a believer; but his father was a Greek. He was well spoken of by the brethren at Lystra and Iconium. Paul wanted Timothy to accompany him; and he took him and circumcised him because of the Jews that were in those places, for they all knew that his father was a Greek.

(Acts 16:1-3)

Paul listed no exceptions to his teaching in 1 Corinthians 7:17-20, but he himself made an exception as we see in Acts 16:1-3. This exception was made after Paul wrote Galatians with its strong words against being circumcised, and also noteworthy, it was just after the Jerusalem Council took place, the Council that decided against the requirement to be circumcised. Also, we do not find Paul making a defense for this circumcision. Therefore, we can know that in 1 Corinthians 7:17-20, even for Paul himself, *menetō* does not mean never; it is conditional and allows flexibility.

The second instance of *menetō* is found in 1 Corinthians 7 verse 24, but we will start with verse 20, the last verse in the previous circumcision example, because it is also part of this context,

*Each person should remain (*menetō)* in the situation they were in when God called them. Were you a slave when you were called? Don't let it trouble you—although if you can gain your freedom, do so. For the one who was a slave when called to faith in the Lord is the Lord's freed person; similarly, the one who was free when called is Christ's slave. You were bought at a price; do not become slaves of human beings. Brothers and sisters, each person, as responsible to God, should remain (*menetō)* in the situation they were in when God called them.* (1 Corinthians 7:20-24)

In this example, Paul says to remain (*menetō*) a slave, but then he gives an exception to his command to remain a slave—the exception is included in these same verses, "…if you can gain your freedom, do so." We see in Paul's slavery example, *menetō* does not mean never; in fact, he meant, if possible, *do not* remain.

Thus we find that by Paul's own usage elsewhere in 1 Corinthians 7, Paul did not mean never by his use of *menetō*; there are exceptions when Paul uses *menetō*. For Paul, in 1 Corinthians 7, *menetō* is conditional.

Paul's Teaching and *Menetō*

Paul made an exception to "remain uncircumcised," and Scripture gives only the briefest glimpse of a reason why Paul might circumcise someone (Timothy, Acts 16:1-3). We get no complete list from Paul for reasons when it might be acceptable to circumcise. Paul makes it clear in his letter to the Galatians that we must not circumcise if it is done to be justified by keeping the law, but other than that, he seems to leave it up to each believer to make the call.

Similarly, for a slave, Paul gives no specifics about how it might come about that a slave might gain his freedom—must he wait until he is freed by his owner? Can the slave himself take steps to gain his freedom? Can the slave purchase his freedom? Can he try to rally a support group to persuade his owner to free him or have others purchase his freedom for him? Again, Paul gives no specifics of how this freedom might be obtained; he leaves it up to the slave.

For each of Paul's uses of *menetō*, we have a Plan A, which is a principle about remaining in a certain situation. We also have the other Plan A, which shows a believer may decide to forgo remaining in the situation.

Paul recognizes and expects there will be exceptions to *menetō*. *Menetō* is conditional in 1 Corinthians 7. If *menetō* allows for a male to be circumcised and a slave to gain his or her freedom, then *menetō* also allows the divorced to remarry. We must find meaning that is contextually appropriate, and we must be consistent in our application.

Appendix E | Sources of Help for Women in Abusive Situations

Immediate Help:

National Domestic Violence Hotline, 800-799-7233 (800-799-SAFE)

Safety Plans:

(It is safer for the woman to download this information from someone else's computer, e.g., using a library or church computer.)

From the American Bar Association—
http://www.abanet.org/tips/publicservice/DVENG.pdf

From the National Domestic Violence Hotline—
http://www.ndvh.org/?get-help/safety-planning
(click on Get Help, and then on Safety Planning)

From the National Network to End Domestic Violence—
http://nnedv.org/projects/safetynet.html

Civic Research Institute—
www.civicresearchinstitute.com/pdfs/DVR1601-SA4-SafetyPlanForAFriend.pdf

Books we recommend:

Lundy Bancroft, *Why Does He Do That? Inside the Minds of Angry and Controlling Men*, 2002

Pastor Jeff Crippen and Anna Wood, *A Cry for Justice: How the Evil of Domestic Abuse Hides in Your Church*, 2012

Jeff and Verla Crippen, *Unholy Charade: Unmasking the Domestic Abuser in the Church*, 2015

Elaine Weiss, Ed.D., *Family and Friends' Guide to Domestic Violence: How to Listen, Talk and Take Action When Someone You Care About is Being Abused*, 2003

Appendix F | Selected Passages Used in This Book

Matthew 5:17-48

Do not think that I have come to abolish the Law or the Prophets; I have not come to abolish them but to fulfill them. For truly, I say to you, until heaven and earth pass away, not an iota, not a dot, will pass from the Law until all is accomplished. Therefore whoever relaxes one of the least of these commandments and teaches others to do the same will be called least in the kingdom of heaven, but whoever does them and teaches them will be called great in the kingdom of heaven. For I tell you, unless your righteousness exceeds that of the scribes and Pharisees, you will never enter the kingdom of heaven.

You have heard that it was said to those of old, "You shall not murder; and whoever murders will be liable to judgment." But I say to you that everyone who is angry with his brother will be liable to judgment; whoever insults his brother will be liable to the council; and whoever says, "You fool!" will be liable to the hell of fire. So if you are offering your gift at the altar and there remember that your brother has something against you, leave your gift there before the altar and go. First be reconciled to your brother, and then come and offer your gift. Come to terms quickly with your accuser while you are going with him to court, lest your accuser hand you over to the judge, and the judge to the guard, and you be put in prison. Truly, I say to you, you will never get out until you have paid the last penny.

You have heard that it was said, "You shall not commit adultery." But I say to you that everyone who looks at a woman with lustful intent has already committed adultery with her in his heart. If your right eye causes you to sin, tear it out and throw it away. For it is better that you lose one of your members than that your whole body be thrown into hell. And if your right hand causes you to sin, cut it off and throw it away. For it is better that you lose one of your members than that your whole body go into hell.

It was also said, "Whoever divorces his wife, let him give her a certificate of divorce." But I say to you that everyone who divorces his wife, except on the ground of sexual immorality, makes her commit adultery, and whoever marries a divorced woman commits adultery.

Again you have heard that it was said to those of old, "You shall not swear falsely, but shall perform to the Lord what you have sworn." But I say to you, Do not take an oath at all, either by heaven, for it is the throne of God, or by the earth, for it is his footstool, or by Jerusalem, for it is the city of the great King. And do not take an oath by your head, for you cannot make one hair white or black. Let what you say be simply "Yes" or "No"; anything more than this comes from evil.

You have heard that it was said, "An eye for an eye and a tooth for a tooth." But I say to you, Do not resist the one who is evil. But if anyone slaps you on the right cheek, turn to him the other also. And if anyone would sue you and take your tunic, let him have your cloak as well. And if anyone forces you to go one mile, go with him two miles. Give to the one who begs from you, and do not refuse the one who would borrow from you.

You have heard that it was said, "You shall love your neighbor and hate your enemy." But I say to you, Love your enemies and pray for those who persecute you, so that you may be sons of your Father who is in heaven. For he makes his sun rise on the evil and on the good, and sends rain on the just and on the unjust. For if you love those who love you, what reward do you have? Do not even the tax collectors do the same? And if you greet only your brothers, what more are you doing than others? Do not even the Gentiles do the same? You therefore must be perfect, as your heavenly Father is perfect. (ESV)

Matthew 19:3-12 and Mark 10:2-12

Matthew 19:3-12 says,

The Pharisees also came to Him, testing Him, and saying to Him, "Is it lawful for a man to divorce his wife for just any reason?"

And He answered and said to them, "Have you not read that He who made them at the beginning 'made them male and female,' and said, 'For this reason a man shall leave his father and mother and be joined to his wife, and the two shall become one flesh'? So then, they are no longer two but one flesh. Therefore what God has joined together, let not man separate."

They said to Him, "Why then did Moses command to give a certificate of divorce, and to put her away?"

He said to them, "Moses, because of the hardness of your hearts, permitted you to divorce your wives, but from the beginning it was not so. And I say to you, whoever divorces his wife, except for sexual immorality, and marries another, commits adultery; and whoever marries her who is divorced commits adultery."

His disciples said to Him, "If such is the case of the man with his wife, it is better not to marry."

But He said to them, "All cannot accept this saying, but only those to whom it has been given: For there are eunuchs who were born thus from their mother's womb, and there are eunuchs who were made eunuchs by men, and there are eunuchs who have made themselves eunuchs for the kingdom of heaven's sake. He who is able to accept it, let him accept it."   (NKJV)

Mark 10:2-12 says,

The Pharisees came and asked Him, "Is it lawful for a man to divorce his wife?" testing Him. And He answered and said to them, "What did Moses command you?"

They said, *"Moses permitted a man to write a certificate of divorce, and to dismiss her."*

And Jesus answered and said to them, *"Because of the hardness of your heart he wrote you this precept.[87] But from the beginning of the creation, God 'made them male and female. For this reason a man shall leave his father and mother and be joined to his wife, and the two shall become one flesh' so then they are no longer two, but one flesh. Therefore what God has joined together, let not man separate."*

In the house His disciples also asked Him again about the same matter. So He said to them, *"Whoever divorces his wife and marries another commits adultery against her. And if a woman divorces her husband and marries another, she commits adultery.*

(NKJV)

Luke 16:1-18

He also said to the disciples, *"There was a rich man who had a manager, and charges were brought to him that this man was wasting his possessions. And he called him and said to him, 'What is this that I hear about you? Turn in the account of your management, for you can no longer be manager.' And the manager said to himself, 'What shall I do, since my master is taking the management away from me? I am not strong enough to dig, and I am ashamed to beg. I have decided what to do, so that when I am removed from management, people may receive me into their houses.' So, summoning his master's debtors one by one, he said to the first, 'How much do you owe my master?' He said, 'A hundred measures of oil.' He said to him, 'Take your bill, and sit down quickly and write fifty.' Then he said to another, 'And how much do you owe?' He said, 'A hundred measures of wheat.' He said to him, 'Take your bill, and write eighty.' The master commended the dishonest manager for his shrewdness. For the sons of this world are more shrewd in dealing with their own generation than the sons of light. And I tell you, make friends for yourselves by means of*

---

[87] The word translated "precept" could also be translated "commandment" or "command."

unrighteous wealth, so that when it fails they may receive you into the eternal dwellings.

"One who is faithful in a very little is also faithful in much, and one who is dishonest in a very little is also dishonest in much. If then you have not been faithful in the unrighteous wealth, who will entrust to you the true riches? And if you have not been faithful in that which is another's, who will give you that which is your own? No servant can serve two masters, for either he will hate the one and love the other, or he will be devoted to the one and despise the other. You cannot serve God and money."

The Pharisees, who were lovers of money, heard all these things, and they ridiculed him. And he said to them, "You are those who justify yourselves before men, but God knows your hearts. For what is exalted among men is an abomination in the sight of God.

"The Law and the Prophets were until John; since then the good news of the kingdom of God is preached, and everyone forces his way into it. But it is easier for heaven and earth to pass away than for one dot of the Law to become void.

"Everyone who divorces his wife and marries another commits adultery, and he who marries a woman divorced from her husband commits adultery. (ESV)

I Corinthians 5:1-13

It is actually reported that there is sexual immorality among you, and of a kind that is not tolerated even among pagans, for a man has his father's wife. And you are arrogant! Ought you not rather to mourn? Let him who has done this be removed from among you.

For though absent in body, I am present in spirit; and as if present, I have already pronounced judgment on the one who did such a thing. When you are assembled in the name of the Lord Jesus and my spirit is present, with the power of our Lord Jesus, you are to deliver this man to Satan for the destruction of the flesh, so that his spirit may be saved in the day of the Lord.

Your boasting is not good. Do you not know that a little leaven leavens the whole lump? Cleanse out the old leaven that you may be a new lump, as you really are unleavened. For Christ, our Passover lamb, has been sacrificed. Let us therefore celebrate the festival, not with the old leaven, the leaven of malice and evil, but with the unleavened bread of sincerity and truth.

I wrote to you in my letter not to associate with sexually immoral people—not at all meaning the sexually immoral of this world, or the greedy and swindlers, or idolaters, since then you would need to go out of the world. But now I am writing to you not to associate with anyone who bears the name of brother if he is guilty of sexual immorality or greed, or is an idolater, reviler, drunkard, or swindler—not even to eat with such a one. For what have I to do with judging outsiders? Is it not those inside the church whom you are to judge? God judges those outside. "Purge the evil person from among you."(ESV)

1 Corinthians 7:1-40

Now for the matters you wrote about: "It is good for a man not to have sexual relations with a woman." But since sexual immorality is occurring, each man should have sexual relations with his own wife, and each woman with her own husband. The husband should fulfill his marital duty to his wife, and likewise the wife to her husband. The wife does not have authority over her own body but yields it to her husband. In the same way, the husband does not have authority over his own body but yields it to his wife. Do not deprive each other except perhaps by mutual consent and for a time, so that you may devote yourselves to prayer. Then come together again so that Satan will not tempt you because of your lack of self-control. I say this as a concession, not as a command. I wish that all of you were as I am. But each of you has your own gift from God; one has this gift, another has that.

Now to the unmarried and the widows I say: It is good for them to stay unmarried, as I do. But if they cannot control themselves, they should marry, for it is better to marry than to burn with passion.

To the married I give this command (not I, but the Lord): A wife must not separate from her husband. But if she does, she must remain unmarried or else be reconciled to her husband. And a husband must not divorce his wife.

To the rest I say this (I, not the Lord): If any brother has a wife who is not a believer and she is willing to live with him, he must not divorce her. And if a woman has a husband who is not a believer and he is willing to live with her, she must not divorce him. For the unbelieving husband has been sanctified through his wife, and the unbelieving wife has been sanctified through her believing husband. Otherwise your children would be unclean, but as it is, they are holy.

But if the unbeliever leaves, let it be so. The brother or the sister is not bound in such circumstances; God has called us to live in peace. How do you know, wife, whether you will save your husband? Or, how do you know, husband, whether you will save your wife?

Nevertheless, each person should live as a believer in whatever situation the Lord has assigned to them, just as God has called them. This is the rule I lay down in all the churches. Was a man already circumcised when he was called? He should not become uncircumcised. Was a man uncircumcised when he was called? He should not be circumcised. Circumcision is nothing and uncircumcision is nothing. Keeping God's commands is what counts. Each person should remain in the situation they were in when God called them.

Were you a slave when you were called? Don't let it trouble you—although if you can gain your freedom, do so. For the one who was a slave when called to faith in the Lord is the Lord's freed person; similarly, the one who was free when called is Christ's slave. You were bought at a price; do not become slaves of human beings. Brothers and sisters, each person, as responsible to God, should remain in the situation they were in when God called them.

Now about virgins: I have no command from the Lord, but I give a judgment as one who by the Lord's mercy is trustworthy. Because of the present crisis, I think that it is good for a man to remain as he is. Are you pledged to a woman? Do not seek to be released. Are you free from such a commitment? Do not look for a wife. But if you do marry, you have not sinned; and if a virgin marries, she has not sinned. But those who marry will face many troubles in this life, and I want to spare you this.

What I mean, brothers and sisters, is that the time is short. From now on those who have wives should live as if they do not; those who mourn, as if they did not; those who are happy, as if they were not; those who buy something, as if it were not theirs to keep; those who use the things of the world, as if not engrossed in them. For this world in its present form is passing away.

I would like you to be free from concern. An unmarried man is concerned about the Lord's affairs—how he can please the Lord. But a married man is concerned about the affairs of this world—how he can please his wife— and his interests are divided. An unmarried woman or virgin is concerned about the Lord's affairs: Her aim is to be devoted to the Lord in both body and spirit. But a married woman is concerned about the affairs of this world—how she can please her husband. I am saying this for your own good, not to restrict you, but that you may live in a right way in undivided devotion to the Lord.

If anyone is worried that he might not be acting honorably toward the virgin he is engaged to, and if his passions are too strong and he feels he ought to marry, he should do as he wants. He is not sinning. They should get married. But the man who has settled the matter in his own mind, who is under no compulsion but has control over his own will, and who has made up his mind not to marry the virgin—this man also does the right thing. So then, he who marries the virgin does right, but he who does not marry her does better.

A woman is bound to her husband as long as he lives. But if her husband dies, she is free to marry anyone she wishes, but he must belong to the Lord. In my judgment, she is happier if she stays as she is—and I think that I too have the Spirit of God. (NIV)

If you have benefited from *Rethinking Biblical Divorce*, please take a moment to post a positive review on Amazon.com.

Even a short message can encourage others to read this book.

Thank you for your support!

The authors gratefully acknowledge speaker and author Anne Miller for taking time out of her busy schedule to edit the text of this book. Her comments and suggestions were invaluable.

Thank you, Anne!

62268250R00126

Made in the USA
Lexington, KY
02 April 2017